The
Heart of England
Way

To my wife Christine

The
Heart of England
Way

WITHDRAWN

Stephen Cross

The Heart of England Way
Association

© The Heart of England Way Association, 2012

Published by Sigma Leisure – an imprint of
Sigma Press, Stobart House, Pontyclerc, Penybanc Road
Ammanford, Carmarthenshire SA18 3HP

British Library Cataloguing in Publication Data

A CIP record for this book is available from the British Library

ISBN: 978-1-85058-908-2

Typesetting and design by: Sigma Press, Ammanford, Carms
All of the maps are reproduced by permission of Ordnance Survey on behalf of HMSO © Crown copyright 2011
All rights reserved. Ordnance Survey Licence number 100048161.

The sponsors of the Ordnance Survey fee ⠿ Turner & Townsend
making the **difference**

The Heart of England Way Association is a member organisation constituted to promote and maintain the Heart of England and Arden Ways, liaise with local authorities and to organise a twice monthly programme of guided walks.

Drawings: © The Heart of England Way Association

Cover photograph: The distant Malvern Hills taken from Meon Hill © Stephen Cross

Printed by: Berforts Group Ltd

Contents

MAP KEY & WAY MARK INDICATORS

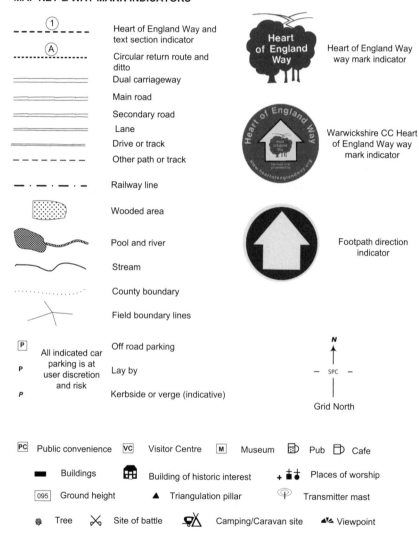

Heart of England Way and text section indicator

Circular return route and ditto

Dual carriageway

Main road

Secondary road

Lane

Drive or track

Other path or track

Railway line

Wooded area

Pool and river

Stream

County boundary

Field boundary lines

All indicated car parking is at user discretion and risk

Off road parking

Lay by

Kerbside or verge (indicative)

Heart of England Way way mark indicator

Warwickshire CC Heart of England Way way mark indicator

Footpath direction indicator

N

SPC

Grid North

PC Public convenience   VC Visitor Centre   M Museum   Pub   Cafe

Buildings   Building of historic interest   Places of worship

095 Ground height   ▲ Triangulation pillar   Transmitter mast

Tree   Site of battle   Camping/Caravan site   Viewpoint

Introduction

This is the first Guide to the 102 mile long Heart of England Way ('the Way' or HoEW) produced by the Heart of England Way Association. The last official guide was produced over 10 years ago, by John Roberts, a great friend of the Association who sadly died in 2009. As editor of our newsletter I volunteered to take on the task of writing this new guide, extended to provide circular walks. Our chairman suggested that a circular walks format should be adopted and I realised that this would extend our walking pleasure by providing 32 individual slices of cake to wet the appetite and reveal the fruit below the icing of the long distance footpath.

Our journey along the Heart of England Way starts in Staffordshire on Cannock Chase and crosses Warwickshire from north-east to south-west, with a little interruption from the western end of Solihull Metropolitan Borough Council, and finishes in North Gloucestershire. As you will read further on, 'the Way' was established as a private venture over 30 years ago, originally terminating at Chipping Campden before being extended to Bourton-on-the-Water.

'The Way' is a 102 mile journey through largely unspoilt English, midlands, shire countryside. It also forms a leg of European Long Distance Footpath E2, which starts in Stranraer and finishes in Nice. We commence our journey on the enormous mound of Cannock Chase; visit Lichfield, as we cross the edge of the Trent Valley, then pass through the Tame Valley. Our journey then negotiates the eastern rim of Birmingham's saucer shaped plateau, then gradually descends through undulating countryside to cross the Avon Valley and the edge of the Vale of Evesham.

Our trails have so far escaped the footprint of the Industrial Revolution, but now we enter the Cotswold Hills, an area untrammelled either directly by industrialisation or by dormitory development to provide homes for those of us who depend upon it. We finish in Bourton-on-the-Water, a tourist honey pot, but throughout our journey we have been able to view the landscape from the 'back door', largely unseen and leaving little trace of our passage.

220 miles is a lot of walking, all of which have been surveyed by me and independently walked and checked by my 'mystery walker' and friend David Higgins. We have both had great enjoyment and hope

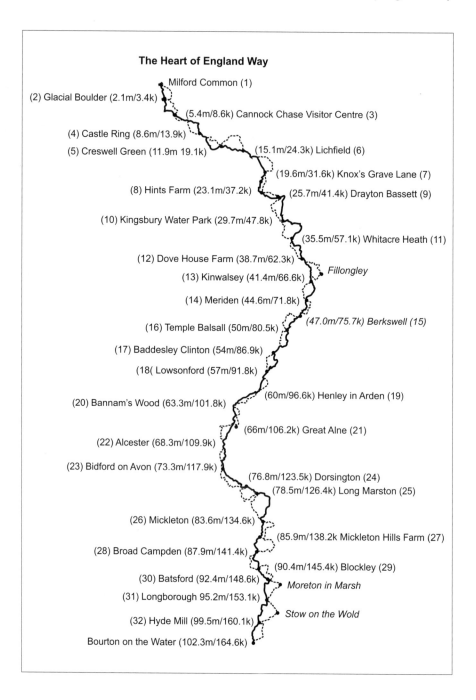

The Heart of England Way

Milford Common (1)

(2) Glacial Boulder (2.1m/3.4k)

(5.4m/8.6k) Cannock Chase Visitor Centre (3)

(4) Castle Ring (8.6m/13.9k)

(5) Creswell Green (11.9m 19.1k)

(15.1m/24.3k) Lichfield (6)

(19.6m/31.6k) Knox's Grave Lane (7)

(8) Hints Farm (23.1m/37.2k)

(25.7m/41.4k) Drayton Bassett (9)

(10) Kingsbury Water Park (29.7m/47.8k)

(35.5m/57.1k) Whitacre Heath (11)

(12) Dove House Farm (38.7m/62.3k)

(13) Kinwalsey (41.4m/66.6k)

Fillongley

(14) Meriden (44.6m/71.8k)

(16) Temple Balsall (50m/80.5k)

(47.0m/75.7k) Berkswell (15)

(17) Baddesley Clinton (54m/86.9k)

(18(Lowsonford (57m/91.8k)

(60m/96.6k) Henley in Arden (19)

(20) Bannam's Wood (63.3m/101.8k)

(66m/106.2k) Great Alne (21)

(22) Alcester (68.3m/109.9k)

(23) Bidford on Avon (73.3m/117.9k)

(76.8m/123.5k) Dorsington (24)

(78.5m/126.4k) Long Marston (25)

(26) Mickleton (83.6m/134.6k)

(85.9m/138.2k Mickleton Hills Farm (27)

(28) Broad Campden (87.9m/141.4k)

(90.4m/145.4k) Blockley (29)

(30) Batsford (92.4m/148.6k)

Moreton in Marsh

(31) Longborough 95.2m/153.1k)

(32) Hyde Mill (99.5m/160.1k)

Stow on the Wold

Bourton on the Water (102.3m/164.6k)

that you do too. However, if you find an obstruction, or have a query, you can contact me by email at editor@heartofenglandway.org. Check also our web site www.heartofenglandway.org for revisions that may have occurred since publication.

How to Use This Guide

For consistency each of the walks is described north to south along 'the Way' (in normal script) and the return route south to north back to the starting point (in italic script). If you decide only to walk the Heart of England Way then you may split the 102 miles into section lengths of your choosing. However, as the route traverses largely rural areas, car parking is not available at all my start/finish points on 'the Way. On the maps I have indicated the parking opportunities and, in the narrative sections, suggested the most practical start point. However, on most walks there is a good degree of flexibility for you to start and finish where you choose, particularly if you are using a Pub!

Each chapter includes a narrative description of the points of interest or 'story' of the journey. This narrative wraps around the individual walks which are formatted with the route directions facing the map of the section.

Along the whole of 'the Way' individual Association members act as wardens for each section of the route, ensuring that our way marks, illustrated on map key page, remain in place and that 'the Way' remains un-obstructed. However on the circular routes, although marked on the OS map as public rights of way, we are reliant on the 'Counties' for providing way marking and directional marker posts in accordance with their statutory requirements. The reality is that there appears to be 'discretion' in some places between the right of way and the route actually established on the ground.

In this guide I have taken a common sense approach and shown the established route, between fixed points e.g. stiles and gates, etc. I have also made the warning note of 'crops' in a very few places where, notwithstanding year on year crop rotation, there was potential for centre field path obstruction where the farmer had left it to the walker to re-establish the path across a field.

At the end of the book I have added some general information including a public transport map. Clearly this information may change, but I certainly added to my own pleasure, when surveying the walks, by using buses and trains to access six sections in South Staffordshire and South Warwickshire.

The History of Heart of England Way

In 2005 it was the 25th Anniversary of the official opening of the Heart of England Way, and I decided to investigate and record the events which lead to its formation. The original idea for the Heart of England Way was born in 1972 when the Alcester Civic Society, responding to a Warwickshire County Council questionnaire concerning footpath use, and wrote their own 'Draft County Structure Plan', for the County's rights of way network. They proposed Master routes, long distance walks across the county, that could join up with other master routes in adjacent counties. One of the routes they proposed was the embryonic Heart of England Way.

Five years elapsed without further word until the Civic Society, in March 1977, contacted Warwickshire County Council to inform them that they intended to carry out a feasibility study to initiate a long distance footpath. The County responded positively with assurances of encouragement and help, notwithstanding their stated 'present financial crisis'.

Following this exchange a new steering committee was formed by John Watts, the originator of the 1972 press release, who invited representatives from seven walking groups along 'the Way'. A route was formulated and, in February 1978, a meeting held with the Warwickshire, Gloucestershire and Worcestershire County Councils together with Solihull Metropolitan Borough Council. Unfortunately the authorities were less than enthusiastic.

Not dissuaded in April 1978, a meeting was arranged with Warwickshire and Staffordshire County Councils, the Country Landowners Association, the NFU and Countryside Commission. However, John Watts reported his disappointment to the Steering Committee: "That both the NFU and the Country Landowners Association see the establishment of a long distance route as a means of closing rights of way and achieving rationalisation of the number of paths". This was clearly noted as not being the intention.

Between April 1978 and August 1979 discussions and meetings took place and promises of action were given, but little progress was made. In frustration the committee decided to throw down the gauntlet and prepare a Guide for publication. In June 1980 a thousand copies of the first Heart of England Way Guide were published. The publicity generated stirred up both wide interest and adverse reactions from councils and landowners. John Watts, responding in the Birmingham Post, stated; "That they had decided to publish a walker's guide to the footpath without recognition or help. We believe that we could have gone on waiting forever...." He was also quoted; "... that only existing rights of way had been used, so there is nothing to stop people using the route". The issue back then was that rights of way were not marked and now, with the original print run sold, potentially there were lot people trying to navigate un-marked footpaths..

During 1981 the Steering Committee achieved some success, working with individual land owners and farmers to remove obstructions and to way mark. By 1982, progress was being achieved; the steering committee had reformed as the Heart of England Way Association, independent of the original walking groups. In Warwickshire, which represented the major stumbling block to progress, they were working with two of the counties divisional engineers, using free issue materials to erect stiles. The Countryside Commission was also working in support of 'the Way' and BBC's *Midlands Today* carried a four minute report of 62 people walking a section of the Way at Meriden.

Finally, in early 1983, John Watts was invited to present the Heart of England Way Development Plan to Warwickshire CC. The Plan recorded the access status, work undertaken by the Association and the work required. The County agreed to review their position and at a meeting of the Transportation Committee, held on the 2nd June 1983, 'acceptance' was achieved. The meeting minute records the statement by the Chairman; "In many people's minds however, the Heart of England Way already exists. It would substantially complete a recognised link between the nationally important Cotswold and Pennine Ways, so now would seem an appropriate time to consider the question of its official recognition by the County Council".

The first sentence of the above quote particularly amuses me, suggesting that many people had only walked the Way in their mind. Perhaps he was ahead of his time; 20 years later we could have avoided all the aggravation and just produced the Heart of England Way as an app! Time rushes by, but local government took until November 1986 to finally conclude that Warwickshire CC,

Staffordshire CC and the Countryside Commission jointly recognised the Heart of England Way as a Regional Footpath. Celebration was perhaps premature as Staffordshire CC, having been invited to join the party, took until May 1988 to formally recognise the Heart of England Way.

The final accolade was achieved on the 13th October 1990; Sir Derek Barber, Chairman of the Countryside Commission, officially opened the Heart of England Way, Warwickshire's first internationally recognised long distance footpath.

I am pleased to record that, since the opening of the Way, relationships between the Association and all parties has been excellent. The partnership has ensured mutual benefit to the walker, landowner, farmer and Councils. Regular meetings with Warwickshire County Council have continued and broadened to serve as the forum providing public consultation on all matters of countryside access. Warwickshire County Council has been a leader in improving footpath access; the Way through Warwickshire has the longest sections of stile free walking.

In 2005, the 25th Anniversary of the publication of the first Guide, the Association recognised the enormous work undertaken by John Watts and his continued contribution to the work of the Association and installed him as Honorary Life President. Trevor Westwood and Brian Keates, Warden Co-ordinator, and original members of the original steering committee are both recognised as Honorary Life Vice Presidents.

Stephen Cross
The Heart of England Way Association

Chapter 1

Section 1: Milford Common to the Glacial Boulder

The first three sections of the Way and the return walks cross Cannock Chase, a unique area, which started its formation 350 million-years ago in the Carboniferous Period. At that time the land lay less than 20 degrees from the equator on the northern edge of what was to become the European land-mass. The Cannock area was an enormous forested, swampy, delta leading to the sea to the north. Over a two million year period alternate flooding and draining laid down a series of layers of coal.

150 million years later the River Budleighensis, flowing along a massive valley from the region of northern France, swept the Chase's second mineral resource onto the area. Over thousands of years, bunter pebbles formed deep surface layers. This ancient geography also explains the enormous salt deposits buried underground in the Cheshire plain, which were then our coastal waters.

Finally, only 20,000-30,000 years ago the ice ages left their mark on the north edge of the Chase. The edge of the Irish Sea Ice Sheet terminated on a north-south line at Brocton, where it is probable that a marginal ice lake formed with glacial spillways forming channels into Sherbrook Valley. One feature the ice age left behind is the large granite boulder in Brocton Field alongside the Way, at the end of Section 1. This boulder apparently came from Dumfries and Galloway, where identical rock strata occurs, and was pushed along by the ice sheet for some 10,000 years before coming to rest on the Chase.

Today, Cannock Chase is part of the largest of the three plateaus, rising to 242m above sea level, which stand in the Midland Triangle. The Midland Triangle itself, is the area bounded by the Pennines in the north, the Shropshire and Herefordshire hills in the west, and the Cotswold hills which run north-east into the Leicestershire hills along the east side. Each of the three corners of the triangle form gateways to the sea. In the south-west the Severn, in the north-east the Trent and in the north-west the 'Midland Gate' leads across the North Shropshire and Cheshire Plain to the Dee and the Mersey.

Since 1920 a large part of the Chase has been managed by the Forestry Commission. Originally planted to provide pit props, nowadays the forest is managed more sympathetically. Its commercial agenda is balanced with environmental and leisure demands; an example of this management was the planting, in 2010, of 4,700 Australian eucalyptus trees. This is part of an experiment to increase the supply of carbon-lean wood fuel in the West Midlands. The Forestry Commission foresters hope the eucalyptus will prove to be more resilient in the warmer weather and wetter summers that we are experiencing, a possible symptom of climate change.

The maps have difficulty in delineating the forest area because it is a working forest; it is subject to constant change. A visit to the Birches Valley Forest Centre (GR 017171) provides more information about their operations and leisure facilities. The Chase has in previous times provided leisure facilities, but not for the masses. In Tudor times it was a Royal hunting forest as well as a source of fuel to feed the Tudor iron industry. By the beginning of the twentieth century it had become an expanse of windswept rolling heath, which was owned by the Earl of Lichfield, whose home lies just to the north at Shugborough Hall.

Today Cannock Chase is unique in many ways. Although it is the smallest area, at 6,880 hectares, designated an 'Area of Outstanding Natural Beauty', it contains the largest expanse of lowland acidic heathland in the Midlands, which in turn is one of the worlds rarest habitats. However, when you add its other habitats which include Sherbrook Valley, Milford Sphagnum Swamp and the several Wet Wooded Valleys, it supports an extra ordinary wide range of flora. The Chase also supports a wide range of birds and mammals including its herds of fallow deer, occasional red deer and the mysterious muntjac.

Our first steps on the Way, lead us from the Milford Common car park through a screen of trees to reveal the authentic face of the Chase. Historic man has not left much of a footprint on the area before the 20th Century. There is some evidence of stone age man, which is referred to later, but it is the deep, man-made cutting, excavated for the Tackeroo Railway, which leads us to the first summit on the Chase.

The railway, long since removed, was laid to serve the First World War Army Camps. The Chase proved an ideal place to establish a base to house the new recruits to Kitchener's armies. Apparently these camps were capable of housing 40,000 men, but very little sign remains of either buildings or the vast infrastructure built to house and train them. The railway line extended from the main line north of the Chase and continued to the West Cannock No 5 Colliery at Brindley Heath, with various branches serving different parts of the camp. The long climb to the first summit emerges onto the open heath land and reaches the now plinth-mounted, glacial boulder.

To return to the start of section 1, turn left from the Way following the gentle decent into Sherbrook Valley, before climbing up the other steep side. The path returns north, passing the old First World War firing-butt embankment, and descends down the green valley to cross the stepping-stones, picnic area and returns to the start.

Walk Directions

1. The Heart of England Way starts at the Milford Common pay and display car park. Go to the end of the car park nearest the A513, climb the few steps and follow the winding footpath through the woods. Emerge in an open area adjacent to a small car park and take the gravel track, initially parallel to the car park access road, and then the left footpath from the marker post. Go up the hill, join a gravel track and back into and through woods on the left to a marker post. At the HoEW signpost turn ¼ left, to follow a track up the gradient of the First World War railway cutting.

2. Turn ½ right at the top of the cutting at a marker post and continue to follow the line of the old railway, steadily rising to reach a tarmac road, adjacent to the car park. Cross the road and continue along the track opposite. Continue to open heath land and take the right fork at a signpost. Follow the track to the summit, adjacent to the trig point on the right, with views of the glacial boulder. The HoEW continues straight ahead along the main path.

A. *To return to the start from the path adjacent to the trig point, continue for 200m along the HoEW to a marker post and take the track ½ left. Follow the track downhill to reach and cross Sherbrook Valley at the stepping stones. Turn left along the track, ignoring the steep track to the right, and continue to take the next track to the right uphill, to reach the summit and the trig point.*

B. *Continue past the trig point to a track junction and turn left along the main track. At end of the First World War rifle range embankment take the track ½ right. Continue across the junction*

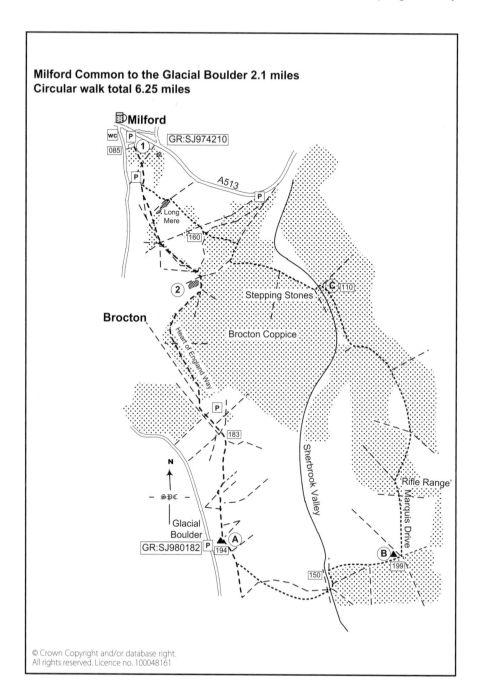

**Milford Common to the Glacial Boulder 2.1 miles
Circular walk total 6.25 miles**

Milford

GR:SJ974210

A513

Long Mere

160

Stepping Stones

C 110

Brocton

Brocton Coppice

Heart of England Way

P

183

N

Sherbrook Valley

'Rifle Range'

Marquis Drive

Glacial
Boulder

GR:SJ980182   P   194   A

B   199

150

and downhill through a long 'glade'. Continue as the track narrows and bends left, to reach an open area and turn right to follow the line of Sherbrook Valley. Continue to reach the main track at a picnic area and turn left.

C. *Cross the brook via stepping stones and turn right at the track junction and continue to the next junction. Turn right along a track to reach the hill summit and a gate on the right, take the path on the left uphill. Reach the top of hill and a junction with a track. Continue straight ahead downhill to the valley bottom and a track junction. Turn left and bear right at Long Mere to rejoin the HoEW, turning right to return to the start.*

Section 2: Glacial Boulder to the Visitor Centre

Now continue south and then turn east adjacent to a café; where we were recommended to try the cream teas, but unfortunately did not have time. The path goes past the Katyn Memorial to 14,000 Polish officers and professionals who were murdered by the Russians in 1940. Further south from this point is the Commonwealth War Cemetery. During the 1st World War 250,000 British and Commonwealth service men passed through the two camps that were built and this cemetery was established for the commonwealth men who died in the camp hospitals. Adjacent is the German War Cemetery, established in 1967, where the remains of all German Servicemen were brought from all over Britain and reburied here.

We continue across the Chase, cross Sherbrook Valley, and re-enter the forest and continue, to reach Marquis Drive and the Visitor Centre. To visit the Visitor Centre we turn right but the return path turns left taking us along a winding path, then dropping down a wide track to Stony Brook.

About 1200m east from here, along the brook, the OS map identifies a 'Burnt Mound' (another exists further south). This is the first evidence of man's 'footprint' on the Chase and arrived during the Stone Age between 10,000 and 4,500BC. Our distant relations, back then, were nomadic hunter-gatherers and the Chase provided ideal summer season provisions. The chase would then have been, much as it is today, bleak in winter but in the summer the wild game would have migrated to the woods and heathland, followed by our ancestors. Their subsistence existence depended on following and killing the game and feeding off the wild nuts and berries, which would have become abundant in the early autumn.

The mounds themselves were their communal ovens and their size indicates that they were used over many years, possibly centuries. They consist of layers of burnt material and heat cracked bunter pebbles. The common aspect between the mounds found on the Chase and elsewhere in the country is the abundance of wood for fuel, adjacent fresh water and the readily available stones. Having no pottery, the game was cooked in the fire or, between the heated stones, or in wooden vessels in which the heated stones were placd to boil the water.

Our return to the boulder stone takes us on mostly forested paths through the Forestry Commission Tackeroo Caravan Site, to cross Sherbrook Valley, and a climb back to the boulder stone.

Adjacent to the Brindley Heath Visitor Centre is the site of the other military camp, which the RAF established during the Second World War. The east side of Brindley Heath was home to RAF Hednesford, or the No. 6 School of Technical Training, as it was officially known. The base continued to operate after the war until the end of National Service, in 1956. Immediately after closing, it was re-opened as a resettlement camp for Hungarian refugees fleeing the Russian invasion. By the 1960s, the site was no longer used and gradually the buildings fell into disrepair before being finally demolished. All that remains to be seen are the roadways and hard standings.

Across on the west side of Brindley Heath was the West Cannock No 5 colliery, which was open between 1914 and 1982. Throughout its life it was blighted by water; nevertheless it was very productive. In the early 1960s its annual output was over 1,000,000 tonnes. However, just before it closed it set a new world record when four seven-man teams tunnelled 251.4 metres in just five days. The area has now been landscaped and trees planted.

Walk Directions

1. From the HoEW main track, adjacent to the trig point, continue along the track to a marker post and take the right track. Continue through an 'avenue' of trees to a marker post in the corner of Chase Road car park and turn ½ right to reach the road. From a marker post take the footpath straight ahead to eventually reach a busy minor road. Turn left back into the forest, along a tarmac road, to the Katyn Memorial and continue along the track. Cross Sherbrook

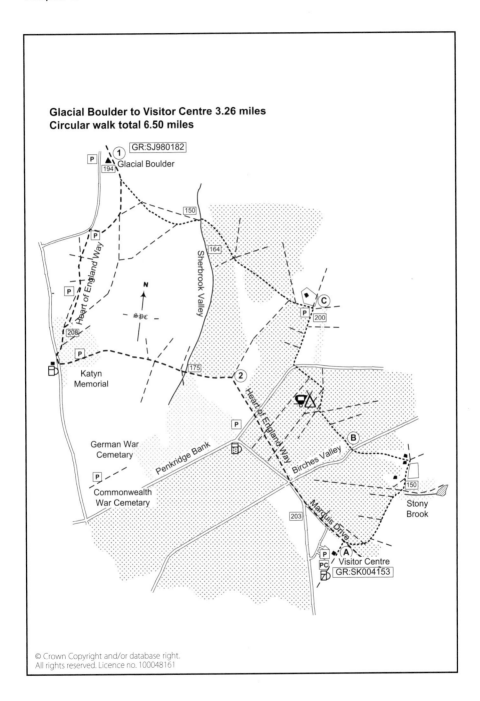

Glacial Boulder to Visitor Centre 3.26 miles
Circular walk total 6.50 miles

Valley and continue along the track. Climb alongside the forest to a junction and take the right fork.

2. Continue along the track to reach the road. Cross the road and continue straight ahead along the path, turning right and left to cross two tracks. At the Birches Valley road, cross the junction and continue along Marquis Drive. Continue past the gates and reach a tarmac footpath on the right, signed Rugeley and Cannock, adjacent to the Visitor Centre. The Heart of England Way continues straight ahead along Marquis Drive.

A. *To return to the Glacial Boulder turn left at the Cannock to Rugeley sign to follow the footpath on the left, signed Rugeley. Follow the footpath as it winds through the trees to reach the open area. Continue downhill with the forest on the left into the valley. Keep straight on following the footpath up hill along the line of the power line. Join a track from the left and continue right to turn left after passing first house. Continue straight ahead to reach and cross the road.*

B. *Follow the wide ride and turn ½ right along the perimeter of a camping and caravan area. Continue to 4-way junction and turn ¼ left, following blue arrows to reach and cross the road. Turn right to follow a wide track and at the barrier turn left and continue through the car park.*

C. *Follow the track straight ahead to drop down into Sherbrook Valley and cross the stream via the stepping stones. Follow the path straight ahead, climbing through the valley, forking right to reach the HoEW. Turn right to reach the Glacial Boulder.*

Section 3: The Visitor Centre to Castle Ring

We now trace the steps that many RAF 'erks' would have made along Marquis Drive and down to the, now closed, Moors Gorse Halt on the Rugeley to Cannock railway line. We cross the railway line at a level crossing, then the A460, before climbing through the forest to cross the Rugeley Road. This last section on the Chase provides the final uphill exertions for some miles as we undulate through two valleys before the final climb to the impressive Castle Ring.

Castle Ring is a hill fort, believed to have been constructed, in about 500BC by the Cornovii tribe. They controlled Cheshire, Shropshire, Herefordshire, Staffordshire and part of Warwickshire and, as we can see this enormous earthwork commanded the highest point, at 235m (766') above sea level, both on Cannock Chase and virtually over anywhere eastwards to the North Sea. Given the tribal nature of the times and the not too pleasant relationships with other tribal kingdoms, the Ring provided an easily defended base for a large number of people. Relationships presumably got better, because it was abandoned before the Romans appeared.

Our return path takes us north along the west edge of the Chase and passes a little distance from the first, and only, unpleasant industrial site along the whole of our walks. After crossing the Rugeley Road we cut through the tip of Beau Desert Golf Club. Beau Desert was established in 1911, within the Staffordshire estate of the Sixth Marquess of Anglesey, Charles Henry Alexander Paget. Although the Marquess reluctantly abandoned his home at Beaudesert Hall and retired to the family home in Anglesey, he remained a great supporter and became the first President of the Club.

After the golf club the path winds down to the A460, circling the Moors Gorse Pumping Station. This is owned by South Staffordshire Water, who provide water to 1.25 million people over an area of 1,490 square kilometres. The company was originally formed in 1853 to provide water to Walsall and Lichfield. Today 40% of the total water supplied by the company is abstracted from over 60 boreholes at 25 sites. The boreholes allow water to be pumped from the Triassic Sandstone aquifer. The Moors Gorse Pumping Station was constructed in 1880.

The return path now allows us to replicate the RAF 'erk' experience, as we climb back up the Way to Brindley Heath and take a diversion around part of the RAF Camp, passing close to the old, now landscaped, colliery site.

Walks Directions

1. From the Rugeley to Cannock path, leading to the Visitor Centre, continue along Marquis Drive, eventually descending steeply to cross a quite busy railway line and then the A460 Cannock to Rugeley road. Cross the A460 and take the track opposite through the lay-by, adjacent to the Moor's Gorse Pumping Station, and ascend the wide track straight ahead. Continue as the track bends

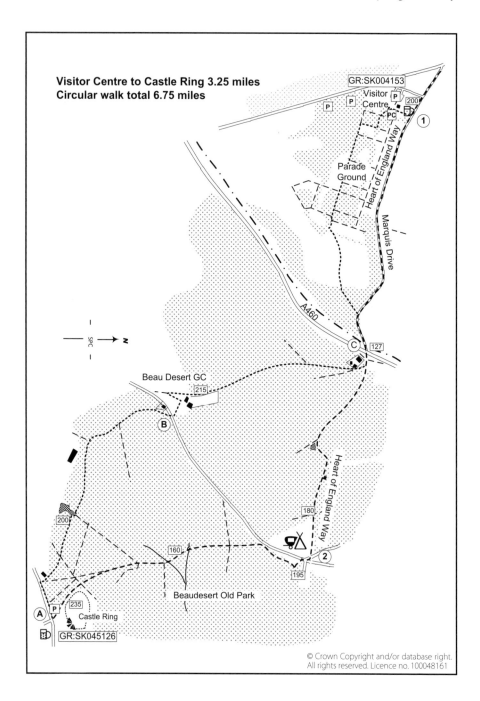

Visitor Centre to Castle Ring 3.25 miles
Circular walk total 6.75 miles

GR:SK004153

Visitor Centre

Parade Ground

Heart of England Way

Marquis Drive

A460

Beau Desert GC

Heart of England Way

Beaudesert Old Park

Castle Ring

GR:SK045126

left and right, as the summit is reached. Pass a gate by houses and continue to reach the road.

2. At the road turn right and then right at a junction, signed Castle Ring. After a few metres take the track left and pass the barrier. Continue to a finger post and turn right and follow the footpath to the road and turn ¾ left to follow a track. Continue along the track downhill and across the valley bottom. After the second stream bear right, and continue climbing to cross a main track. After 400m take a small path ¼ left, if clear, and follow along the path to continue below the summit of Castle Ring. If the small path is missed, turn left at a five-way junction, as the ground levels, and then right at the next path, to continue below the summit of Castle Ring and reach the car park.

A. *To return to the Visitor Centre from the car park, turn right along the road and then right, adjacent to a house, to take the left fork of the track. Follow this track straight on downhill and pass the end of a pool. Continue straight on, bending right as the track climbs to reach and cross Rugeley Road.*

B. *Take the Beau Desert Golf Club drive opposite and turn left adjacent to the car park. Continue along the track to a hut and turn ¾ right to follow a track alongside the 18th green, noting advice regarding golfers! Follow this track straight ahead, passing a barrier and gradually descending to join a track from the right, passing houses on the left. Continue downhill to join the HoEW and turn left to cross the A460 Cannock to Rugeley road.*

C. *Re-trace the HoEW route, climbing Marquis Drive, until reaching a right hand bend and take the footpath left. Follow the footpath through the wooded area, then across open heath forking left, and then through band of trees to reach a corner of the old RAF Camp road system. Continue straight ahead along the road past the open area on the right, the old parade ground, to then take the second road right. Take the next path left and follow it to the Visitor Centre.*

Chapter 2

Section 4: Castle Ring to Creswell Green

As soon as we leave the Chase we pass the first Pub along on the Way, The Castle Ring and, like 'buses', with no pub for the first 9 miles this section provides a further three: the Windmill, the Drill Inn and the Nelson Inn at the end of the section. The return route passes close by the Malt Shovel, which provides an all day welcome in its bars and coffee lounge.

As we leave the road and enter a path we walk along the side of another South Staffordshire Water pumping station. The route through Gentleshaw passes Christ Church, with its castellated tower, and the Windmill Pub next door. The diversion right from the road takes us onto Gentleshaw Common.

Like Cannock Chase this is an area of lowland heath extending over 86 hectares and is a Site of Special Scientific Interest (SSSI) and a grade 1 Site of Biological Importance. Because of its status, there is an ongoing programme to restore this part of the critical heathland link across Staffordshire and prevent further fragmentation of the existing heathland sites. The ongoing work sees the felling of regenerating scrub and the containment of bracken by grazing or gathering. These heathland management practices have been carried out on Gentleshaw for thousands of years, ensuring that the nutrient poor soil environment is not enriched by invading species and that the natural heathers and bilberries survive.

A large proportion of mature birch and rowan have been retained for the significant landscape value that they hold. The success of the work, according to Staffordshire County Council, is reflected in the return of uncommon birds, such as short eared owl, woodlark and nightjar gradually returning to the area.

As we descend the common, the first and one of the few views along the Way of the West Midlands conurbation is revealed. From the common we enter the agricultural countryside first farmed by the Saxons. The attraction of the land to the early farmers was the easily obtainable fresh water resource available from springs or shallow wells tapping the gravel beds of the Chase aquifer, apart from Maple Brook emerging from the Chase.

The only evidence remaining of Saxon habitation are today's local names. Hednesford derives its name from the Ford of Heoden, Stafford from Staeth Forda meaning 'the Ford at the Wharf'. Cannock itself is possibly derived from the Celtic word 'cnoc', meaning high place, which describes it very well as it sits on the southern edge of the Cannock Chase outcrop. Possibly this indicates that the town of Cannock was inhabited even before the Romans.

The return from the Nelson Inn climbs back to the summit of Castle Ring crossing twice through the steep valley of Maple Brook which starts its journey from a spring just below Castle Ring.

Walk Directions

1. From the Castle Ring car park bear left along Holly Hill, behind the Park Gate pub. Continue to the junction and cross Chestall Road, to take the gate and follow the footpath, then turn right along a surfaced drive and take the footpath straight on, just before road. Join the road and continue straight on past the school and into Common Side. At a power line pole take the footpath on the right along the edge of Gentleshaw Common. Follow the footpath, which continues close to the edge of the common, ignoring paths going right. After 1500m, at the end of the common, join the road at the cross roads. Turn right and cross the road to take the stile.

2. Follow the left hedge through 2 fields and at the 2nd stile go right to cross the bridge and double stile then turn left to follow the left hedge. Take the stile and turn left along the lane. Pass the Drill Inn and reach a T-junction. Cross the road and carry straight on along the bridleway. Continue to the end of the bridleway at the junction with a lane and turn right and then left at next junction to reach The Nelson Inn at Creswell Green.

A. *At the bridleway junction with the lane turn left. Continue along the lane and just after Hillside Farm at a gap in the hedge on the right take the stile. Cross the field, take the stile and continue to the hedge corner on the right. Turn ¼ right downhill and cross the field through a line of trees to a bridge. Cross this 'sloping' bridge with care and follow the right hedge up hill and take the stile then field gate on the right. Turn left to follow the left hedge and take the gate to the road.*

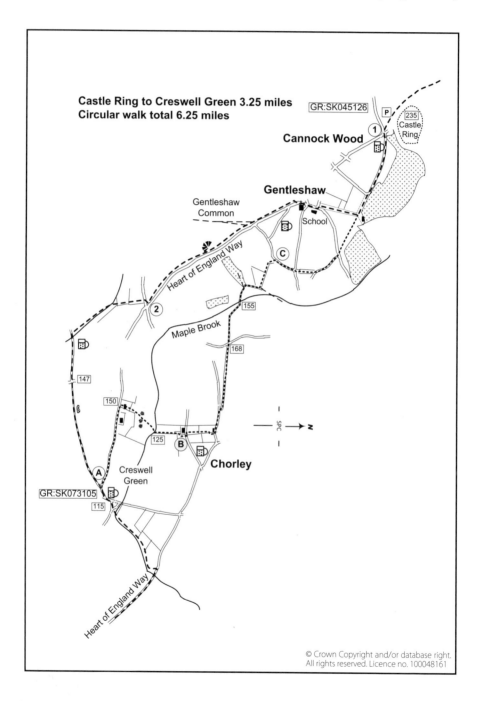

Castle Ring to Creswell Green 3.25 miles
Circular walk total 6.25 miles

GR:SK045126

Cannock Wood

Gentleshaw

Gentleshaw
Common

School

Heart of England Way

Maple Brook

Chorley

Creswell
Green

GR:SK073105

B. *Turn left and take the stile on right and follow the right hedge. Take 2 stiles then the gate on right, turn left, follow the hedge and take the stile to the road. Turn left along the road taking the right fork along Dodds Lane to a T-junction. Cross straight over at the junction and follow a path along a green lane over a brook. Continue uphill, pass a path on the left, as the green lane bends right, and continue to reach and take the stile on left. Follow the right hedge uphill, take a stile and continue with the hedge, turning right to take a stile to the road.*

C. *Turn right downhill along the road, turn right at the junction and take the stile immediately on the left. Follow the left hedge, take a stile and continue along a wide path and take 2 gates to reach the road. Turn left uphill and straight over at T-junction to take a gate. Cross the field ¼ left to the corner and take the gate. Continue straight ahead back along the HoEW to return to the Castle Ring car park.*

Section 5: Creswell Green to Lichfield

We continue to Lichfield through fields alongside Maple Brook, a short distance along a quiet lane and more cross-country. We now join Abnalls Lane, descending a holloway on the approach to Lichfield and pass an impressive building complex, entitled the 'Abnalls'.

This name dates back to 1318 when a house and virgate at Abnalls were held at Farewell Priory by Roger of Abnall. However by 1357 the estate, consisting of a messuage, a mill, a carucate, and other land in Abnalls, Pipe, Elmhurst, and Lichfield was held by Nicholas Taverner, described as parson of Stretton. The various estates passed through many worthy hands through the centuries but Roger appears to have left his stamp.

Just further on where we turn right from the road there is the impressive entrance to the hidden Maple Hayes, a Grade II listed building. The present building was originally built in 1794 as a manor house by George Addams, a Lichfield wine merchant. Addams built the house of three storeys, with five bays, a central porched entrance, and with single storey wings in a plain Georgian style.

In 1884, Albert Octavius Worthington, of the famous Burton on Trent brewery Worthington & Co, bought the house. He extended the estate and enlarged and much improved the house in about 1884. The estate was broken up and sold in 1950. In 1951 the house was acquired by Staffordshire County Council and sold in 1981 becoming the Maple Hayes School for Dyslexics.

Whilst Cannock Chase has evidence of Ancient Britons living off the land 4000 years ago, it was not until after the Romans disappeared, having effectively built the Lichfield by-passes of Watling and Ryknild Streets, that Lichfield entered the history books, with the arrival of Bishop Chad in AD669.

Chad, born of noble parents in Northumbria in AD623, became a pupil of the Venerable Bede, as did his three brothers. Bede sent him to Ireland to widen his education with the religious scholars from where he returned to take over, on his brother's death, the monastery he had established at Lastingham in Yorkshire.

Chad had obviously made his mark as the King of Northumbria, deciding that he should become Bishop, sent him off to be ordained. His journey became somewhat extended, not only because he insisted on emulating the apostles and going everywhere on foot, but he went first to Kent then to Dorchester to find a Bishop to conduct the ceremony. No sooner had he returned, and been installed as Bishop of York when the Bishop of Mercia died, so he was transferred there. This time his journey was made more quickly, as he was physically lifted onto a horse and forced to ride.

Although the bishopric seat was at Repton, Chad decided to move the seat closer to the Royal Palace at Tamworth. He chose the holy site of Licidfelth, which translates as 'Field of the Dead', in honour of the butchery of 1000 British Christians. Having put Lichfield on the map and established his church on the present cathedral site, his tenure was short lived as he died on the 2nd March AD672. Perhaps, given his insistence on walking everywhere, he should be adopted as the Patron Saint of the Heart of England Way.

After St Chad the settlement quickly grew as an ecclesiastical centre, which was consolidated in the 12th century by Bishop Clinton who fortified the Cathedral Close and laid out the town in a ladder-shaped street pattern. The Bishop could perhaps be charged with self interest as the church owned the land and rents were payable to the Bishop.

Lichfield continued to develop, establishing the Guild of St Mary and John the Baptist in 1387, with the construction of the Guild Hall in Bore Street, which is still there today. In 1553 the city achieved greater status when Queen Mary enacted a Charter, which granted Lichfield County status. The office of Sheriff of Lichfield, which was created then, is still retained.

Lichfield Cathedral

Like many established centres of population the civil war did not pass Lichfield by. Strategically situated on the north-south divide, it became a royalist stronghold. The parliamentarians gave the cathedral no respect, desecrating it in 1643 and returning in 1646 to bombard it, collapsing the central spire. In 1662, following the appointment of Bishop Hacket, the rebuilding of the cathedral was undertaken with vigour, which was further enhanced in the Victorian era.

At the start of the 18th Century, the city had once again regained its status as an attractive centre to live and was considered by learned society to be the best town in the area for good conversation and company. The wealth of the clergy and the gentry in the Cathedral Close generated prosperity, intellectual culture and the grand attractive buildings we see today.

There are many famous Lichfieldians either born in the city or immigrants, like Joseph Addison (1672-1719), drawn there because of the church. His father was Dean of Lichfield and the young Addison, who was educated at the city's grammar school, became one of the 18th century giants of literature. Addison wrote poetry, essays, plays as well as being a political journalist. He is buried in Westminster Abbey.

Predating Addison was Elias Ashmole (1617-1692) born and educated in Lichfield. He became a lawyer working in London but moved to Oxford at the start of the Civil War where he kept in contact with the royalist armies in Lichfield. After the war he moved back to London where he was rewarded for his loyalty to the Crown and made Windsor Herald. After the death of his first wife he married a much older, but rich, lady and was able to use her wealth to pursue his passion in astrology, magic, botany, alchemy and other scientific studies to form an important collection of manuscripts.

Despite his interest in magic he was a founder member of the Royal Society. In 1675 he began arrangements to hand over his vast collection of manuscripts and documents to Oxford University, where they were housed in a new museum, the Old Ashmoleum which was completed in 1683. Ashmole always remembered his Lichfield roots and the cathedral has several music manuscripts and a beautiful silver drinking vessel, the Ashmole Cup.

Perhaps the most famous old Lichfieldian was Dr Samuel Johnson, born in 1709; he died in 1784 at the house on the corner of the Market Square and Breadmarket Street. Although his parents were beset by financial problems he was educated at Lichfield and Stourbridge Grammar Schools and a short-lived term at Oxford. Having no luck entering a teaching career he drifted into a writing and a career in journalism, working in London and in Birmingham, where he met his wife to be.

They tried to set up a school outside Lichfield, but failed and moved to London. After several years of hack writing he was offered the major job of compiling an English Dictionary. This brought him fame but little money until the government granted him a £300 a year pension. His fame brought him friendship with the famous, including James Boswell and Joshua Reynolds, which masked his fear of solitude and anguish. On his death he was buried in Westminster Abbey, a national celebrity. The Samuel Johnson Museum is in the corner of Market Square, entry is free.

Our return to Creswell Green leaves the Cathedral Close via a series of paths and around a very pleasant, residential area to reach Dimbles Lane. We continue to cross Eastern Avenue where the path is deemed 'open to all traffic' but, after crossing Circuit Brook, Fox Lane becomes a quiet footpath entering the equally quiet hamlet of Elmhurst.

Between the A515 and A51 the path takes us through and around fields which do not appear to have much footfall.

After the A51 we set off for Farewell, its name, of Saxon origin, meaning 'clear spring', which derives from the Anglo Saxon 'frager' meaning clear and 'wiell' meaning spring. We take an easy path to 'Cross in Hand Lane' and around a field edge to the small church of St Bartholomew. The lane is believed to be so called because the village was the site of a Benedictine Priory and travellers requiring sanctuary there would have approached with a cross in their hand. The present church was rebuilt in 1745 although the alter rails, glass in the east window and Miserere stalls are 13th century. From the church we pass a large barn and continue across the field, possibly having to separate crops and vegetation, and climb up to the village of Chorley.

Walk Directions

1. Pass the Nelson Inn, turn right at the road junction and then straight over at the T-junction. Take the footpath over the footbridge and take the stile on the left. Now follow the brook at the edge of the field, take 2 stiles and then take the stile to a lane. Turn right along the lane and continue into and left along Little Pipe Lane. At the bend, adjacent to Keeper's Cottage, turn left up the bank to take the stile. Cross the field ½ right, to take the stile and continue, to take another stile. Continue straight ahead to follow the fence on the right and take a stile. Continue with the right hedge, take the stile/gap and cross the field ½ left, to take the stile. Continue across the next field ½ right, to take the stile and turn left along the lane.

2. Follow this sometimes busy narrow lane for 750m, to just past the entrance drive of Maple Hayes Hall. Immediately after this entrance take the footpath on the right and take the gate. Follow a wide sweeping path turning left with the fence/hedge. Cross a brook, and turn left to take the gate. Cross the field to reach, then cross, the A51 and take the stile. Follow the right hedge, take the stile and cross a track and follow the footpath, turning right at a fence. Continue around the perimeter of the golf course for 400m and turn left through the 2nd car park into Shaw Lane. Follow Shaw Lane, turn right along Beacon Street and left into the Close and the Cathedral.

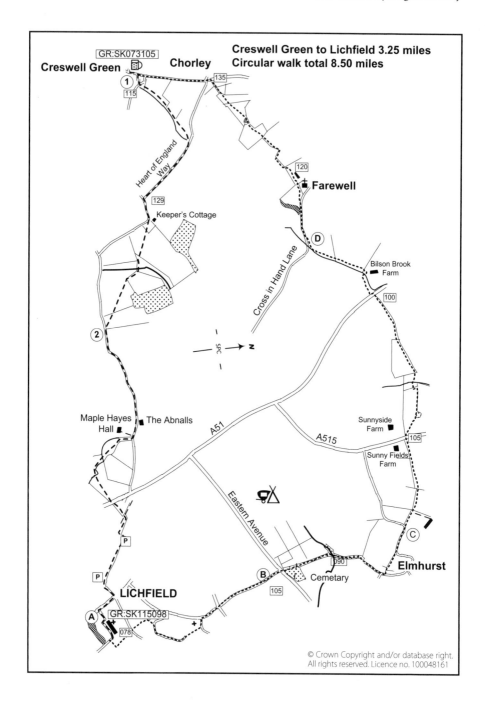

Creswell Green to Lichfield 3.25 miles
Circular walk total 8.50 miles

GR:SK073105
Creswell Green   Chorley
1
115
135

Heart of England Way

120
Farewell

129
Keeper's Cottage

Cross in Hand Lane

D
Bilson Brook
Farm
100

2

SPC → N

Maple Hayes   The Abnalls
Hall   A51   A515   Sunnyside
Farm
105

Sunny Fields
Farm

Eastern Avenue

P

P
LICHFIELD   B   C
GR:SK115098   090   Elmhurst
A   105   Cemetary
078

A. *Continue along the Close, to turn right into Dam Street, 1st left into Reeve Lane and then 1st left along Bishop's Walk. Cross a lane and continue along the footpath to meet a road and turn right and follow the footpath to reach Gaiafields Road. Turn right, follow the road and take a continuing footpath to reach, and turn left along, Dimbles Hill, adjacent the Church. At the junction with Dimbles Lane turn right and follow the road to its junction with Eastern Avenue.*

B. *Cross Eastern Avenue and take the footpath steps. Follow the wide footpath, cross a track and continue straight ahead alongside a cemetery. Turn right to cross a brook and follow the footpath which becomes a sunken green lane and then a road. Follow the road to just after a road junction and take a footpath left between the houses, take the stile and cross the field with the left hedge, then take the stile and turn left along the lane.*

C. *As the lane bends left, take the track straight ahead. Leave the track as it bends right and keep straight ahead to take the stile. Follow the left hedge/fence through 2 fields and take the stile to the A515 road. Cross the road to the left and enter a field through a hedge gap. Cross the field ¼ right to the trees and turn left downhill along the old field boundary to reach a gate in the hedge corner of a field on the left. Either take the gate or follow the hedge left to reach and take a stile on the right. Having entered the field cross the brook via the bridge then continue ½ right across the field to take the stile. Follow the right hedge/brook through 2 fields and take a stile to reach A51. Cross the road left to turn right along a farm drive to a yard. Turn right, cross over the brook and turn immediate left alongside the brook. Follow the brook through 2 fields to reach and turn right along a lane.*

D. *Follow the lane for 250m and take the stile on the left. Go right around the field, pass a church and up the bank to take the gate. Follow the track, pass the house, to the marker post. Go left down the bank and follow the right hedge/fence to the next post and turn right. Follow the left hedge around the field and through a gap to the next field. Cross the field on line of 2 trees, then straight on with the hedge, pass a pond on the left and cross the field ¼ left to take the stile by a tree. Cross the field ½ left, take the corner stile and follow the path to the road. Turn left and continue straight over junction to return to the Nelson Inn.*

Chapter 3

Section 6: Lichfield to Knox's Grave Lane

To start this section of the Way, leave the Cathedral Close and walk along the peaceful pedestrianised Dam Street, as good an aspect as you will find in any market town, made even more impressive by the view across Stowe Pool. Continuing through the market square, we pass the church of St Mary and St John the Baptist and its adjacent Guild Hall. After the impressive building housing Boots, the route continues through a modern shopping precinct and then leaves the town centre to wander through housing estates to reach the A51 Tamworth Road.

Just after the 'Horse and Jockey', the Way joins a footpath going straight ahead for 2½ miles over the gentle dome of Packington Moor to the green thoroughfare of Knox's Grave Lane. After some research, I discovered that Mr Knox was a late 18th century highway man who attacked solitary travellers late at night with his cudgel. Seemingly one night he had been particularly lucky and robbed a man of his pistol, powder and shot.

Now armed, he decided to move up the criminal hierarchy and stopped a mail coach demanding the mail box. This was his undoing, as four army officers were on board returning from leave. He panicked, failed to fire the pistol and was captured and within three days was tried and hung. His parents, it is believed, reclaimed the body and buried him close to their cottage which was somewhere, now unknown, in the lane.

At the lane 'the Way' continues right and we return to Lichfield with a left turn and pass an active area of gravel extraction. After turning left across the fields, we cross the A51 and enter the ancient woodland of Hopwas Hays. We continue over the natural uncultivated sandy soil to cross Staffordshire Regiment's firing range.

The Staffordshire Regiment was an amalgamation of the separate North and South 'Staffords'. Both regiments can trace their history back to early 18th century and the oldest was raised by Colonel Lillington as the 38th Regiment of Foot at Lichfield. The 'Staffords' were amalgamated into the Mercian Regiment in 2007 as the 3rd armoured infantry battalion, and are based in Germany. The firing range is little used, but check the telephone number on the map. The museum is also well worth a visit.

The path returns to Lichfield via the aptly named Sandy Lane and alongside the Whittington Golf Course to the A51.

Walk Directions

1. Continue along The Close to the right of the Cathedral and turn right into Dam Street. Continue into Bakers Lane through the shopping mall and at the end turn left and right to Birmingham Road. Cross over and continue along Levetts Fields turning left to cross the railway via the bridge on the right. Follow the footpath to reach and cross Cherry Orchard right and continue along Oakhurst to No. 45 and take the footpath right. Cross Manor Rise and continue along the footpath straight ahead to Hillside. Turn right and follow Hillside to Borrowcop Lane and turn left. Turn right into Quarry Hills Lane and left along the Tamworth Road (A51). Cross the A51 and continue for 1100m, passing the Horse and Jockey and at the end of a brick wall take the footpath right.

2. Take the gate, follow the right hedge, cross a field, take the gate and follow the track/bridleway straight ahead all the way to Knox's Grave Lane. Pass Freeford Home Farm, take the pedestrian gate and cross the track to Ingleyhill Farm and continue between the fence and hedge. Take the gate, and follow the line of the less well used track straight ahead via 2 gates to reach and cross Jerry's Lane. Continue straight ahead along the bridleway to reach the main cross bridleway of Knox's Grave Lane.

A. *Turn left and follow the bridleway, take the farm gate and continue with the right hedge and ignore a signed diverted bridleway. Join a vehicle track, bend left at the gravel workings and turn left beside the access road. At a gate take the left stile and follow a fenced footpath to the A51, via a stile and steps. Cross the road at the lay-by and take the track opposite to a junction and turn left to follow the right fence. Bear left at the track junction and continue straight on to join a track from the left, take the gate, bear left exiting the woods.*

B. *Continue along the track at the side of the rifle range* until just after the brook and turn ½ right to pass the end of the next firing butt.*

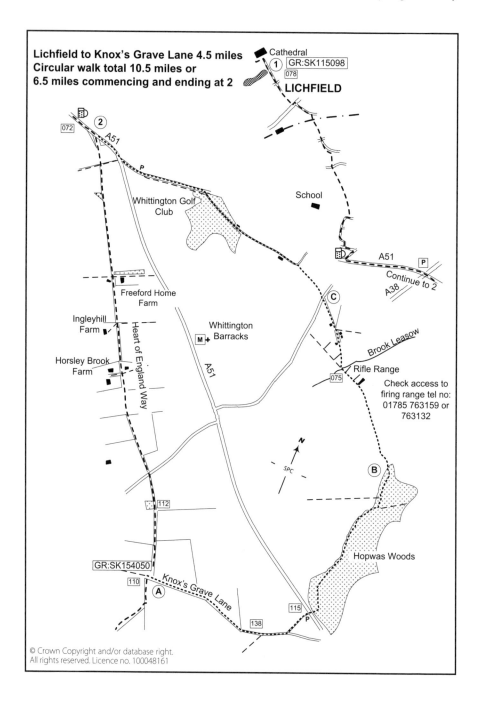

Lichfield to Knox's Grave Lane 4.5 miles
Circular walk total 10.5 miles or
6.5 miles commencing and ending at 2

Cathedral
① GR:SK115098
078
LICHFIELD

072
②

A51

Whittington Golf
Club

School

A51
P
Continue to 2
A38

Freeford Home
Farm

Ingleyhill
Farm

Heart of England Way

Whittington
M Barracks

A51

C

Brook Leasow

Rifle Range
075

Check access to
firing range tel no:
01785 763159 or
763132

Horsley Brook
Farm

N
SPC

B

112

Hopwas Woods

GR:SK154050
110
Ⓐ   Knox's Grave Lane

115
138
P

Continue across the open area to walk between the lines of two hedges and reach a track at a bend. Continue straight ahead along the track taking the gate to the road.

C. *Cross the road and enter the field opposite and continue straight ahead to take the stile to Sandy Lane. Continue straight ahead along the lane to reach the road. Turn left along a somewhat busy road and rejoin the A51 just before a large lay-by. Turn right to point 2 or the centre of Lichfield.*

* The MOD rifle range has limited use but check that access is available via telephone 01785 763159 or 01785 763132.

Section 7: Knox's Grave Lane to Hints Farm

From the lane we soon pass under the 'new' A5, which opened in 2005. The old Watling Street Roman road remains, and a cohort of legionnaires could probably walk along it relatively undisturbed today. We now enter a 13km^2 triangle of quiet farm land scattered with woods. The climb to the top of Crows Castle is delightful and it is perhaps difficult to imagine the view when, and if, the route of the proposed high speed train to London is built exactly on this line!

This area formed the Canwell Estate and was purchased by Birmingham Corporation after the First World War to provide homes and work for heroes. By the early 1920s the estate, totalling over 4,000 acres, consisted of 140 small holdings and 150 buildings including 15 farm houses, 63 houses and 48 cottages. The city had also provided over 6 miles of road together with water and drainage services, although mains electricity was not installed until 1950.

Farming was mainly milk production but there was also arable and market gardening on the estate. According to the city's records, at the estates zenith in 1949, there were 1,388 head of cattle, 74,000 birds, 420 pigs and 73 horses – half the number that were utilised in the 1920s. The land today is all privately owned but it is still possible to imagine it during its earlier days. In Birmingham's day they also owned the Basset's Pole Inn, and the name of Basset can be traced back to Norman times.

In the late 11th Century Hugh I, Earl of Chester, produced an illegitimate daughter, named Geva, who, despite her questionable antecedents married well. She produced a daughter Maud who also did well marrying a Richard Basset. Geva must have been a well thought of woman, for when she decided to establish a Benedictine Priory at Canwell her grandson Ralph Basset gave his assent. The Priory was dedicated to St Giles with the foundation being for the 'souls of herself, her ancestors, and her kinsmen' and as made 'by the authority of Bishop Roger of Chester'.

Unfortunately the estate, compared with other priories, was poor and in 1524 Cardinal Wolsey dissolved it, along with 20 other church estates, to fund his project to establish Cardinal College, Oxford. The land passed through the hands of several local families before Birmingham bought it.

Why Geva founded her priory here is possibly due of the prescience at the northern end of the estate of the site of the ancient St Modwen's well. An early description of the well states that it "was aluminous and famous for unaccountable cures of divers ailes and weaknesses".

From Hints Farm our return route once again crosses the quiet fields of the estate before we re-cross Black Brook, on its way to the River Tame. We now wander through the hamlet of Hints, passing the small church of St Bartholomew. This 'modern' building, built in 1883, was designed by John Oldrid Scott, the younger son of Sir George Gilbert Scott, one of the leaders of the Gothic Revival movement. From Hints we return via Watling Street and alongside the gravel workings to return to Knox's Grave Lane.

Walk Directions

1. At Knox's Grave Lane turn right along the hedge and take the gate on the left. Follow the right hedge for 200m and turn right through a gap. Follow the left hedge, which joins a farm track, and continues into a road and bridge over the A5. Go through the farm yard then left of the house and reach the B5404 and turn right. After 80m take the drive on the left and take the stile then bear left at a fork in the drive, cross the bridge and take the stile. Continue straight ahead with the left hedge, take the stile and cross the field passing the edge of a wood and take the stile.

2. The path now climbs Gorsey Hill, aim towards the dip in the saddle and over the ridge to take the stile. Continue with the right fence, take the stile and turn left and follow the track to a lane at Rookery

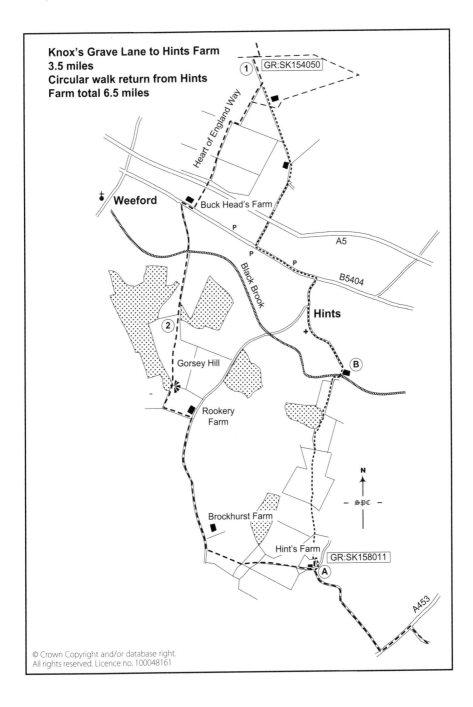

Knox's Grave Lane to Hints Farm
3.5 miles
Circular walk return from Hints
Farm total 6.5 miles

1 GR:SK154050

Heart of England Way

Weeford

Buck Head's Farm

P

A5

P P

Black Brook

B5404

Hints

2

Gorsey Hill

B

Rookery
Farm

N

Brockhurst Farm

Hint's Farm

GR:SK158011

A

A453

Farm and turn right. Follow the lane and just past Brockhurst Farm turn left through a gap in the hedge. Cross the field aiming for a lone tree just over the hill, to take the stile. Turn ½ left, cross the field to take the stile, follow the right fence and take the stile to a lane at Hints Farm.

A. *Immediately after Hints Farm take the stile on the left and follow the left hedge, then ½ right to cross the field to take the stile and footbridge in the field corner. Cross the middle of the field towards a marker post and the large trees, then aim right of the pylon to take the hedge gap. Turn left follow the left hedge and edge of wood. Take 2 stiles on the left through the corner of the wood. Follow the right hedge and take 3 stiles and turn right alongside Black Brook and take the stile at a farm building and turn left.*

B. *Continue through the farm yard and cross the bridge to join School Lane. Follow the lane through the village of Hints passing St Bartholomew Church and turn left along the B5404. Continue for 600m and turn right into the lane signed Hints Quarry and under the A5. Continue to the right bend and adjacent to the brick buildings turn left along the bridle path. At Buck's Head Cottages the path bends left and right then continues straight ahead taking a gate to Knox's Grave Lane.*

Section 8: Hints Farm to Drayton Bassett

Following the official route of the Way we continue along Bangley Lane and turn left along the busy Sutton Road, then right to follow Drayton Lane to the village of Drayton Bassett. There is an alternative route which, as I explain in the route description, involves walking a surfaced lane that is privately owned. We will continue to raise the matter with Staffordshire County Council.

I am afraid that this first and sizable village after leaving Lichfield has no shops or pub! The lack of a pub can be blamed on Sir Robert Peel (1788-1850), although the residents have a Working Men's Club. Peel, who lived in the village, was MP for Tamworth and had a long career in government including a term as Prime Minister. Historically his major claim to fame was his founding of the London Metropolitan Police which is why the British policeman is known as a 'Bobby'. Robert's father migrated from Lancashire and acquired the Manor of

Drayton and later Robert had the Drayton Manor house built.

The Peel family determined that no pub should be built in the village so we may wonder how they would feel about their home and park being host, since 1975, of the ever expanding and successful theme park.

Evidence has been discovered which establishes that Drayton Bassett has had people living close to the church since around the 1100s. The present church, apart from the tower, which probably dates from the 13th century, was rebuilt during the Peel eras and extended when Robert was interred there after his death.

Walk Directions

Since the creation of the Heart of England Way the route has followed Drayton Lane, a long section of sometimes busy road, without a footpath. There is an alternative well walked, cross-country, right of way route to reach Drayton Bassett, but the final approach is along Heathley Lane, which, although not a public road, is walked regularly by local people. The adoption of this lane has been a priority in the Staffordshire CC 'Right of Way Improvement Plan' for many years, of which the Association continues to remind them.

Paragraph 1 describes the prescribed route of the Heart of England Way along Drayton Lane.

Paragraphs A and B (east) and C (west) describe the cross-country route via the private Heathley Lane in both directions. When I walked the lane paper signs, in plastic bags, warned dog walkers that the lane is private.

1. From Hints Farm, to follow the route of the official HoEW, turn right along Bangley Lane to reach the A453 and turn left. After 350m turn right into Drayton Lane and continue to Drayton Bassett and turn left at the junction with Salts Lane to reach the church of St Peter.

A. *From Hints Farm turn right into Bangley Lane and immediately turn left to go through a gap in the hedge. Cross the field, passing left of the right power pole to reach the edge of the field to the left of a tree and take the bridge over the ditch. Cross the field, take the stile and follow the right hedge continuing to take the stile and bridge. Cross the field ½ left to the far corner and take the stile and fenced footpath between properties to the A453*

Hints Farm to Drayton Bassett via Drayton Lane 2.60 miles
Hints Farm to Drayton Bassett via cross country route 2.33 miles

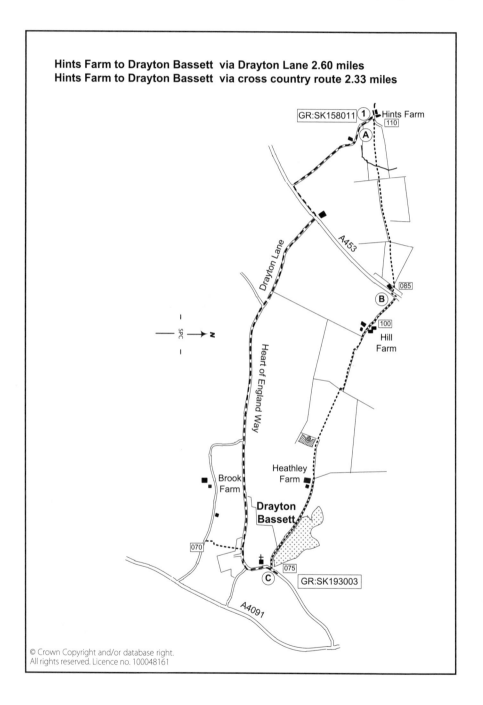

B. *Turn left and then right to take the lane through gates to Hill Farm. At the farm access continue right and left between the farm buildings and industrial unit. Pass the barriers and take a pedestrian gate at a double farm gate. Continue straight ahead along the left side of the field and through a gap in the hedge. Cross the field and continue to Heathley Farm between the stream and embankments. Join Heathley Lane, pass around a pair of gates and continue to Drayton Bassett.*

C. *From Drayton Bassett take Heathley Lane and pass the farm and at the right bend in the lane continue straight on with the right hedge/stream. Cross the field, aiming for the farm buildings in the distance, through the hedge gap and continue straight ahead with the right hedge to take the stile. Follow the track, take the pedestrian gate, pass the barriers and follow the surfaced drive between farm buildings and industrial unit to reach the A453. Cross the road, turn left for 50m and take the footpath right. Take the stile, cross the field ½ left to the corner and take the bridge and stile. Follow the left hedge, take the stile, cross the field and take the bridge. Cross the field centrally to the right of the left power pole to reach the corner gap in the hedge and Hints Farm.*

Section 9: Drayton Bassett to Kingsbury Waterpark

Leaving the village we continue to cross the A4091 and, via an amusing castellated bridge, cross and join our first canal – the Birmingham and Fazeley Canal. Agreement to build this canal, which we follow south, was made in 1782. Unusually, for the times, co-operation was obtained from other companies to build this missing link to the Trent and Mersey, Coventry and Oxford and Birmingham Navigation Canals, enabling goods to be transported to all parts of the English canal network.

We turn off the canal to enter Warwickshire County Council's jewel, Kingsbury Water Park, which opened in 1975. The whole of this area, part of Bodymoor Heath, has been subject to gravel extraction for decades. Since 1975 the park has expanded; today, as the gravel has been worked out, it has 15 lakes covering 600 acres of landscaped park. This sustainable environment not only provides habitat for wild life, but leisure facilities for water sports and angling. Its many miles of paths attract everyone from the family stroller, wildlife enthusiast, to the serious health fanatic. Access to the park for visitors on foot is free with a reasonable charge made for car access to its many car parks. The 2km long loop of the Echills Wood Miniature Railway, run by enthusiasts, is also very much worth a ride, whatever your age!

The HoEW continues east through the park to return to Drayton Bassett; we exit via the main entrance, joining Bodymoor Heath Road. Just before crossing the canal we could take a diversion left to the canal-side pub, the Dog and Doublet. After leaving the road we cross fields and reach the impressive Aston Villa FC Academy and Training Ground.

At a marker post there are two alternative routes; either turn left and go largely cross-country to Middleton, or continue along a permissive path to reach Middleton Hall. This area is the centre of major land restoration, part of the Central Rivers Project – an initiative aimed at boosting river wildlife in the Tame Valley. Hanson Aggregates has partnered with the local community and the RSPB in this 10 year project, which has reintroduced reedbeds, field ponds, meadows, marshland and woodland, all of which had disappeared, mainly due to changes in agriculture. Today it is a lost haven for wildlife with otters, a large variety of birds, insects and fish, which have been re-introduced.

All of this area surrounds the three buildings that make up Middleton Hall. The oldest part was built in 1285, and was the first house on the Manor of Middleton. The next phase was the Great Hall of Tudor origin, built around 1530, and the stable block was late Tudor. More modifications were constructed in 1650 and in 1720 the main west wing was added when the owner was elevated to the peerage. The south wing was added in the early part of the 19th century. The building lay derelict for many years before the Middleton Hall Trust was formed, raising funds to rescue and restore the property.

If you have chosen to visit Middleton Hall then take the entrance drive, cross the A4091 and walk along the busy lane to Middleton. The alternative cross-country route from the marker post is a pleasant walk through fields and a wood.

The village of Middleton has a pub, the Green Man, which is very popular, particularly at weekends, and is close to the church of St John the Baptist. Its church tower would prove an ideal place to train spot, should the High Speed Railway be built, as it will pass 300m from the village on an 18m high embankment.

The church, having probably been a Saxon place of worship, was originally Norman and was extended in the 13th and 15th century. More recent repairs, to remove the decaying, Victorian plaster, revealed the remains of 14th century wall paintings, created before the walls were limewashed, as they would have been in the middle ages. We now cross the fields and the Warwickshire - Staffordshire County borders, at the footbridge, to return to Drayton Bassett.

Walk Directions

1. From St Peter's Church continue along Salts Lane to reach the A4091, Tamworth Road. Cross the busy road and via the bridge with its tower and spiral staircases cross the canal and turn right. Follow the canal for about 3.5km and take the parallel footpath just before the lock buildings.

2. Follow the wide surfaced footpath as it turns to the left, before the buildings. Continue following the path right alongside Canal Pool, then Broomey Croft Pool. At the end of the pool turn left past the car park and continue to reach and turn right to follow Gibson's Road alongside Cliff Pool South, then bear right beside Gibson's Pool. At the main path junction, turn left and follow the Information Centre signs under the motorway, then turn right to follow the winding woodland path. This path crosses the miniature railway adjacent 'Wrens Tunnel'. Turn right and follow the railway passing 'Picnic Junction'. The footpath continues to reach and cross a surfaced road, turn right, cross the bridge, bear right and cross the railway. Turn left through the station car park and then right to reach the Information Centre.

A. *From the Information Centre go to the road entrance and turn right along Bodymoor Heath Road. Follow the road over the canal and in another 550m take the gate on the right and follow the edge of field path. At the end of the field turn left to cross the field, take the gate cross the road, take next gate and cross the entrance road to the impressive Aston Villa Academy and Training Centre. The path now continues along the centre of a narrow tree plantation turning right and crossing a plant access route to the adjacent gravel workings.*

B. *50m after the plant crossing turn ¾ left, at a way mark post, to follow a marked footpath and reach a fence. Continue left, between the*

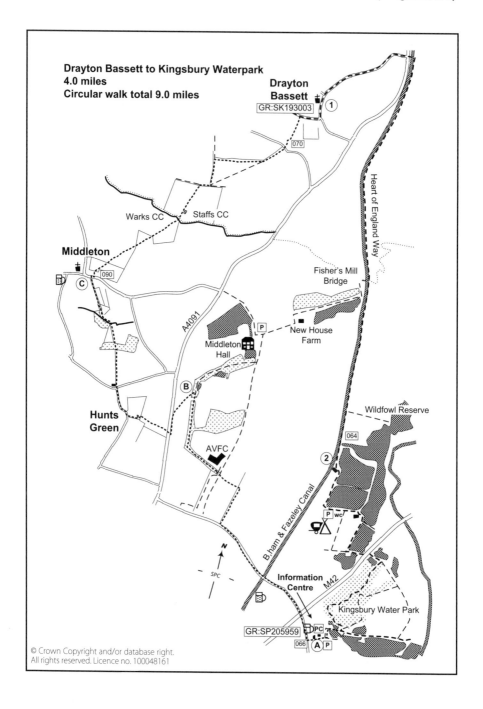

Drayton Bassett to Kingsbury Waterpark
4.0 miles
Circular walk total 9.0 miles

Drayton Bassett
GR:SK193003 (1)

070

Warks CC   Staffs CC

Middleton
090
(C)

Fisher's Mill
Bridge

A4091

New House
Farm

Middleton
Hall

(B)

Hunts
Green

Wildfowl Reserve

064

(2)

AVFC

P wc

Information
Centre

M42

Kingsbury Water Park

SPC

GR:SP205959   P C

066 (A) P

fence and an embankment, to reach and take the gate on the right. Cross the A4091 take the gate, cross the field, take the gate by a power pole, cross the bridge, take the gate and turn left. Follow the left hedge around the pool and continue around the field to take the bridge and gate to the lane. Turn right along the lane to reach a road junction, cross straight over to take the footpath on the right of Park House drive. Follow the left hedge and continue through the wood, take the gate then follow the left fence to take the bridge. Turn left follow the brook then edge of the wood leading to a fenced footpath. Continue past a bungalow to reach Middleton, close to the Green Man pub.

C. *Turn right for a few metres and take the footpath left, up steps, to reach and cross the recreation area ½ right. Take the gate and continue ½ right on the same line to cross through 3 fields, taking 2 hedge gaps to reach and take the bridge. Continue ahead for a few metres and take the track passing left of a tree/pond and cross this usually cultivated field. Take the hedge gap and turn right along a track and left along next track. At a hedge on the right, turn right, to follow the hedge around the field to take the stile to a lane. Cross the lane and take a gap in the fence, cross the field and follow the path between the houses to Drayton Lane and turn right along the HoEW. Turn left at Salts Lane to return to the church.*

Chapter 4

Section 10: Kingsbury Water Park to Whitacre Heath

From the Information Centre we walk north-west alongside the main water sports lake.

As we leave the park we cross the River Tame, which is described as the most urbanised in the country. The river starts as two streams which join together in Walsall. From there it flows mostly through a man-made channel providing the main drain for the West Midlands conurbation. Under spaghetti junction (M6 junction 5) it picks up the River Rea, and later, east of Birmingham, the Rivers Cole and Blythe. However, as we cross the river, it has had the benefit of flowing through the Lea Marston settlement and purification lakes. From our crossing point it does sustain fish life, as it continues to join the river Trent 41 miles from its source.

We now climb the steps at the side of Kingsbury Hall. The name Kingsbury, means a fortified place, and the hall is probably on the site of the original defences. The hall has been in disrepair for many years and was owned by the Bracebridge family for four centuries from the 12th century. The village remained quite small, from the time of its Saxon origins, but grew in size when coal mining was established in

Kingsbury Church and Manor House from the 'Way'

the area and later as a dormitory to Birmingham. We pass by the 12th century church of St Peter and St Paul, which is described by some as one of the finest in the county.

Leaving the village we pass under the 'Birmingham – Derby' railway line, which opened in 1839, then the road to Kingsbury Oil Terminal, the largest inland facility in the UK, watch out for road tankers! We now negotiate a rifle range and navigate our way across an enormous cultivated prairie field to Camp Farm. We have now climbed the eastern 'saucers lip' around the edge of the Birmingham plateau, along which we meander as far as Chadwick End.

At Foul End, apparently it means 'muddy land', we continue off road for about 1¼ miles to reach Whitacre Heath and the railway line again. However this line is now only a little used branch off the mainline, which goes directly from Kingsbury to Birmingham. The line was built by the Birmingham Derby Junction Railway Company (BDJR) to provide a link via other company's railways between Gloucester via Birmingham to the North East.

However at the same time another company, the Midland Counties Railway (MCR) was constructing a line linking Derby and Nottingham with Rugby. Both the BDJR and the MCR connected with the London Birmingham Railway (LBR) at Birmingham and Rugby respectively. Although both the BDJR and the MCR had routes that complemented each other, they both had ideas for additional branches which would lead to both fighting each other for the North of England – London business.

The MCR intended a branch north of Nottingham, which would divert traffic from the BDJR business and the BDJR intended to provide the Whitacre branch to Hampton in Arden, providing a quicker route to London than via Birmingham.

Parliamentary guidelines forbid the development of competing railways so both the BDJR and the MCR reached a gentlemen's agreement to not develop the two branches. However the MCR reneged on the deal and at the last moment included their branch in their application to parliament, so BDJR submitted a separate bill to parliament for their Hampton branch. It was not surprising that the BDJR bill was successful, as MP, Sir Robert Peel, was a member of the BDJR Board.

The BDJR opened their line to passengers in August 1839, ten months ahead of the MCR. The first train from Birmingham to London took seven hours for the 135 mile journey. For ten months it had the monopoly of Derby London traffic. But with the opening of the MCR a shorter route cutting about half an hour off the journey to London was available. A tariff war ensued. Writs were served by both sides and lost. Both the MCR and BDJR faced crippling losses which each were prepared to suffer, as long as the other side's was greater.

The outcome of this war was that the shareholders, many of whom had investments in all of the local railway companies, pressed for amalgamation. In May 1844 both the MCR and the BDJR were merged with the North Midland Railway to form the Midland Railway. Effectively this meant the end of the branch through Whitacre to Hampton, which perhaps holds the record of being the most short-lived railway line. The line between Whitacre and Hampton ceased effective operations in 1877, although to meet statutory requirements a daily single passenger train ran until 1917.

The White Swan pub is just the other side of the railway and, along the road, through the village another 200m is the Railway Inn. To return to Kingsbury Waterpark we take the Birmingham Road opposite the White Swan to eventually cross the main railway line and the River Tame. Just after, a footpath takes us behind Severn Trent's installations serving the river's settlement lakes. After negotiating the large roundabout a right turn in Marston takes us along the original route of the Kingsbury Road, which clearly would not have been fit for today's road tanker traffic.

We follow a series of footpaths through the Waterpark to arrive back at the Visitor Centre.

Walk Directions

1. From the Information Centre take the footpath and cross the road towards the car park and turn left into the miniature railway car park. Pass the station and at the end of the car park turn right. Follow the footpath, cross the railway line, then bridge and continue alongside the lake to reach and cross the steel footbridge left. Follow the footpath over the River Tame and continue up the steps, pass the church and continue along the footpath through the left side of the cemetery. Turn right to join the Coventry Road, passing the Royal Oak Pub, and continue for 250m to take the footpath on the left between the houses. Take the footbridge and follow the path at the rear of the houses and under the railway. Turn right and left alongside the ditch and cross the road.

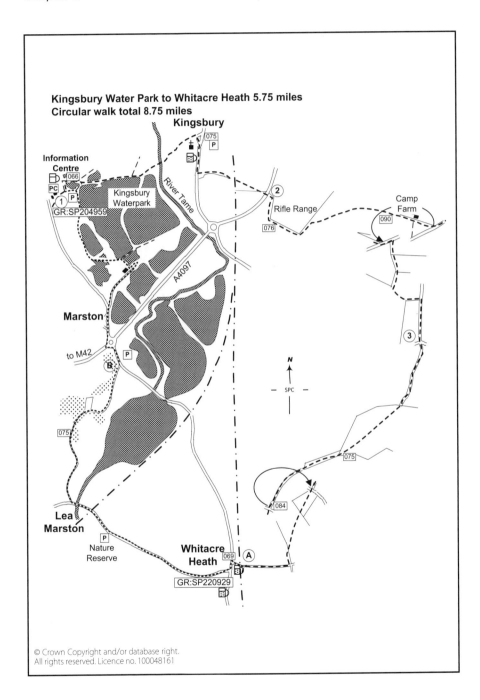

Kingsbury Water Park to Whitacre Heath 5.75 miles
Circular walk total 8.75 miles

Kingsbury

Information
Centre

GR:SP204959

Kingsbury
Waterpark

River Tame

A4097

Rifle Range

Camp
Farm

Marston

to M42

N

SPC

Lea
Marston

Nature
Reserve

Whitacre
Heath

GR:SP220929

2. Follow the left field edge and turn right at the range perimeter. Keeping in the fields continue over the access road turning left to go behind the huts and left again, at the second corner, along the other side of the range. Continue for 100m and at the marker post turn ½ right to cross the field, climbing the slope to aim for a tree. Continue right with the left hedge to reach and keep straight ahead along the lane. At the road junction turn left and after 75m take the gate on the right. Follow the right hedge and after the 2nd stile continue to the end of the hedge at a marker post. Continue ½ left across the field, follow right hedge and turn right along the lane.

3. At the T-junction cross straight over to take the track. Follow the track to reach an open field. Cross the field ½ right, take the gate and follow the stream to take the gate, to join a track then drive. Follow the drive to reach and cross a road and the take stile opposite. Cross the field, take the stile, cross the field ½ left take the gate, follow the left hedge and take the gate to a road. Turn right along the road and at the approach to a bridge (to continue the HoEW) turn left in front of a bungalow and continue to turn left along the track alongside the railway.

A. *Continue along road over the railway bridge and turn left, passing the White Swan Pub, and right into Birmingham Road. Follow the road crossing the railway line and the River Tame. Take the bridleway right, at the Environment Agency Purification Lakes sign, and continue for 1300m to reach and turn left along Coton Road.*

B. *Keeping straight on negotiate the roundabout to reach Marston and turn right into Kingsbury Road. Continue along the road, past the houses on the left. 50m after the road becomes a track turn left and back alongside the pool. Turn right between pool and the fence and join the surfaced drive. Turn left and take the footpath ½ right from the corner of the drive. Follow the footpath around the lake and rejoin the surfaced track, adjacent to the Information Centre and car parks.*

Section 11: Whitacre Heath to Dovehouse Farm

Following the track at the side of the railway line, we continue through open fields, to cross the road at the quaintly named hamlet of

Hoggrill's End. The next field takes us to the railway that should be crossed with care.

We now turn left along a path between the railway line and the hidden Shustoke Reservoirs. The reservoirs, fed by the River Bourne, were built in the 1880s to serve Birmingham. However, as soon as Birmingham finished its project to obtain water from the Elan Valley, in the early 20th century, The Shustoke waters were diverted to Nuneaton and Coventry. The reservoir capacities are 92k and 1.92m cubic metres. The large reservoir has a sailing club and the adjacent car park is a useful free facility.

After passing alongside a short section of the River Bourne we hook around the woods at the end of the smaller pool and turn left to reach the road. However, just before the road a path left could provide a diversion to the Griffin pub and the adjacent St Cuthbert's Church. After the road we continue cross-country, climbing again the plateau lip with views to the right, on a clear day, of the near hump of Coleshill and the more distant spreading vista of Birmingham. After crossing a stream and going through the pretty Dumble Wood, the return route turns right and the Way continues left. Continuing along the Way through Dumble Wood to the lane; you may spot, on the right, the overgrown quarry that would have provided the reddish brown stone for the original buildings in the area.

Returning to Whitacre Heath our path follows the edge of the wood right and left, re-crosses the stream and through the fields to reach Shustoke and the Plough Inn. Shustoke has Saxon origins but the village here has little evidence of this as the original centre was adjacent to St Cuthbert's Church and the Griffin Pub.

Turning left along the road, we pass the reservoir car park, and take a footpath which still shows the remains of its tarmac surface from the days when it lead to Shustoke's railway station and the abandoned Hampton in Arden branch. After crossing the railway we continue, via field paths, passing an interpretation board for the Colin Teall Woods and ignoring the ancient 'UTMD' warning sign of the long since abandoned sewage works to reach Whitacre Heath.

Walk Directions

1. Pass the bungalow and turn left along the rail-side track to its' end and take the gate. Follow the left hedge, cross a bridge continue ½ left across the field and take the stiles and bridge. Turn right with

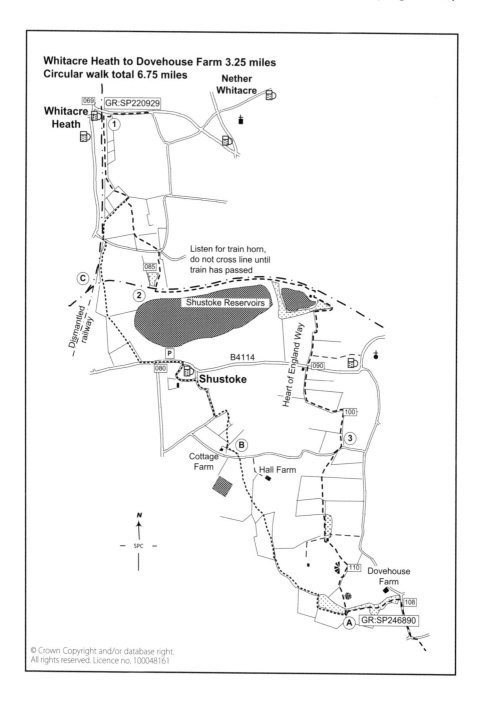

Whitacre Heath to Dovehouse Farm 3.25 miles
Circular walk total 6.75 miles

Nether Whitacre

069   GR:SP220929

Whitacre Heath

1

Listen for train horn, do not cross line until train has passed

085

C

Dismantled railway

2

Shustoke Reservoirs

P

080

B4114

090

Shustoke

Heart of England Way

100

3

B

Cottage Farm

Hall Farm

N

SPC

110   Dovehouse Farm

108

A   GR:SP246890

the hedge then at the ditch turn left to follow the ditch, through a hedge gap. Continue ½ left across the field to the corner. Take the stile, cross the road left of Hoggrills End Lane sign and take the stile. Follow the fence then cross the field to follow the right edge of the wood to cross the railway.

2. Turn left along the rail-side path, for 1400m then turn right to pass a house. Follow the stream-side track, pass the 'Severn Trent Welcome' sign and follow the fence on the right, cross the bridge, take the gate and turn right. Follow the field edge to the corner and turn left with the hedge on right to continue to and reach the B4114. Cross the road, take the gate and follow the right hedge, take the gate and continue to the 2nd gate (on right) to turn left to follow the right hedge. Take the gate on the right and follow the left hedge through a gate and on to take a gate to the road.

3. Turn right for a few metres and at the bend take the hedge gap on the left. Follow the left hedge, take the stile and cross the field. Take the gate, cross the field left of a large tree and take the gate. Follow the left hedge, take the bridge, follow the edge of the wood, pass the barn and cross a track ½ left. Follow the left hedge then on the same line cross the field and turn right with the hedge (views to Birmingham). At a post turn through the hedge gap and cross the field right of a tree. Cross the bridge, take the steps then through a copse to take a gate. To continue along HoEW turn left to take a gate, follow the left field edge and take a gate into a wood. Follow the footpath to the lane and turn right.

A. *Take gate from copse, turn right, continue around the right field edge and turn right through 2 gates. Follow the right field edge, take the stile and bridge, then turn left and follow the field edge for 500m and take the stile on the left. Turn right with the ditch and at the 2nd ditch crossing turn ½ left and cross the field. Take the gated bridge and continue ¼ right across the field to take the gated bridge. Cross the long field ¾ right (crops) to take the gate into a lane.*

B. *Turn left along the lane for a few metres and take the gate on the right. Turn ½ left to reach a marker post, cross the bridge and take the gate. Turn right with the field edge, take the gate and cross the field ½ left, to take the gate. Follow the left hedge, join a drive turning left to the road. Turn right along the road, then left into Back Lane. At the B4114, adjacent to the Plough Inn, cross the road and turn left along the footpath for 300m. Take the footpath right, to the left of Sewage Treatment access, and via a partly surfaced path take the stile and cross the field. Take the bridge, cross the field take the stile and cross the railway and take the stile.*

C. *Follow the fenced footpath, take the stile adjacent Colin Teall Wood information board, and continue with the left hedge. Take the stile, turn left along road and at the railway bridge take the stile on the right. Follow the left fence, through a hedge gap and turn right with the right hedge, pass a 'warning sign' turn right over a bridge, turn left and cross a bridge joining the HoEW and take the stile on the left. Cross the field ¼ left, cross the bridge, continue with the right hedge to join the rail side track and return to the start.*

Section 12: Dovehouse Farm to the Kinwalsey

At the lane adjacent to Dove House Farm turn right. There are fairly wide verges along the lane but, if you walk the circular path, you may choose to start and finish in Fillongley.

Leaving the lane we walk for about 900m around the perimeter of an enormous field. When I walked it, in early spring, two separate herds of fallow deer, some distance from each other, were feeding off the green shoots of the cereal crop. They watched warily as I approached and, before I could get within suitable photo opportunity distance, first one herd then the other made its escape to Shawbury Wood. We now weave our way through a more traditional landscape of small fields, adjacent woods and streams draining the contoured landscape.

After a short distance along the narrow Fillongley Lane we cross more mixed farming to reach Barrat's Farm. The Way continues between the farm buildings and can be very 'soft'. Across the fields the distant hum becomes a roar as we cross a bridge over the M6. We are again at the top of the plateau rim, as the traffic pours beneath us through the cutting. This is the best vantage point to see across the plateau and the 10 mile distant centre of Birmingham.

The return route to Dove House Farm is back through Barrat's Farm, where we turn right along the lane to reach and cross the Meriden Road. We now follow a farm track alongside a pleasant unnamed stream, which we eventually cross, and pass the tree covered 'Ring and Bailey'. Entering Fillongley at its centre we find the Manor House Pub, some shops and the 12th century church of St Mary and All Saints. The origins of Fillongley's name is Saxon meaning 'clearing of Fylga's people'. There is some kerb side parking in Church Lane.

We climb out of Fillongley and join a footpath which goes through the Fillongley Cricket Club, close to the Cottage Inn. We then take Mill Lane and follow a footpath along the valley of the River Bourne. Looking ahead we can see the Daw Mill Colliery, which is the single largest coal producing mine in the UK.

The coal is in a seam 5m thick known, as the 'Warwickshire Thick', some 750 metres below the ground. The mine workings were established in 1957 and it is envisaged that coal reserves, which extend beyond the M6, will continue to be worked until 2028. In 2008 it beat a 13 year old record for annual production by producing 3.25 million tonnes. The rest of our walk is along more of the same traditional countryside, sprinkled with woods.

Walk Directions

1. Continue along the lane to a junction, turn left and take the gate immediately on the right. Follow the right perimeter around this vast field to take the gate on the right adjacent Shawbury Wood. Follow the edge of the wood through a hedge gap and cross the field ½ right, take the right gate to a lane. Turn left along the lane, pass the junction with Hardingwood Lane and take the gate on the right.

2. Cross the field to a marker post and continue with the left hedge to a marker post and cross field ¼ left. Take the stiles and bridge through a thicket and turn right with the right hedge. Take a stile, cross the field ½ left, take the stile, cross the field to take a stile. Cross the lane, take the stile and continue ¼ right across the field to take a stile. Follow the left fence, pass the house and join the track to the road.

3. Cross the road into Gorsey Green Lane and take the gate on the left. Cross the field, take the gate and continue ½ right to take a gate to a lane. Turn left and right to the entrance of Barrat's Farm and take the gate on the right. Turn ½ left to take 2 gates between the barns and straight ahead to take a gate into the field. Cross the field, take the gate and continue ¼ left to the M6 Bridge.

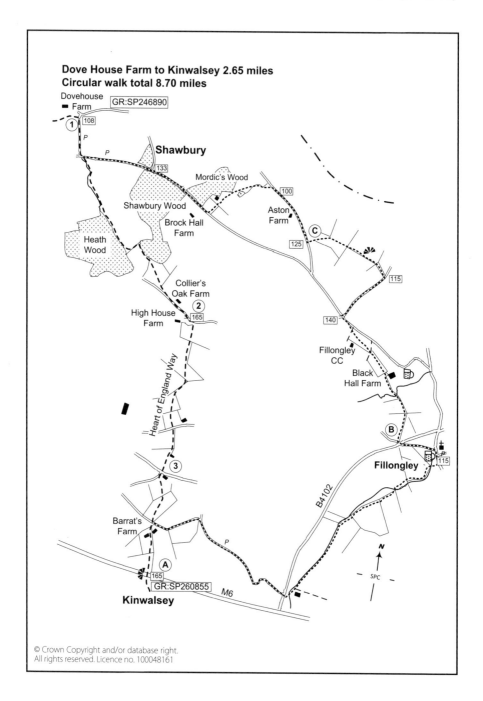

Dove House Farm to Kinwalsey 2.65 miles
Circular walk total 8.70 miles

Dovehouse Farm
GR:SP246890
1 108
P
P
Shawbury
133
Mordic's Wood
100
Shawbury Wood
Aston Farm
Brock Hall Farm
C
Heath Wood
125
115
Collier's Oak Farm
2 165
High House Farm
140
Fillongley CC
Black Hall Farm
Heart of England Way
B
3
115
Fillongley
B4102
Barrat's Farm
P
A
N
165
SPC
GR:SP260855 M6
Kinwalsey

A. *From the M6 return through the farm to the lane and turn right. Follow the lane to reach and cross over the Meriden Road. Take the stile and turn left along a track then right across the stream and turn left to follow the stream at the edge of the field. Continue to reach and follow a hedge on the left through 2 hedge gaps and cross the bridge on the left. Cross the field ½ right, take the stile and follow the right hedge as it bends left, ignore a metal gate, and then take a gate/stile and follow the footpath up the steps to take a stile and follow a drive to the road. Turn left past the Manor House Pub and the Church of St Mary's then turn left up Ousterne Lane.*

B. *Cross over Meriden Road into Pump Lane and take the gate on the right and follow the right hedge. Take the gate, cross a stream and bear left to follow the right hedge, take a stile and cross the field. Take a gate, cross the track right and left, take the steps and gate and cross the field ½ right. Cross Fillongley Cricket Club drive via the 2 gates and continue to the field corner. Take the gate and turn left along the lane. Turn right down Mill Lane for 450m and take the gate on the left and follow the path between the fences and take the gate. Follow the left fence take the gate and cross the field (crops) to the corner of the hedge and turn ¾ left up the field to a marker post at the end of a bank. Continue on the same line to a lane and turn right.*

C. *Continue for 500m along lane through a valley and take a gate on the left adjacent an electricity pylon. Cross the corner of the field ½ right to a hedge corner, continue through a wide hedge gap and follow the right hedge and take the gate on the right. Cross the field ½ left (crops) to the corner of Mardic's Wood and a marker post. Cross the field to the left of a barn, take the gate, continue with the left hedge and take the gate to Shawbury Lane. Turn right along the lane pass the Shawbury sign and continue straight ahead down Cow Lane to meet the Heart of England Way and turn right for Dove House Farm.*

Section 13: Kinwalsey to the Queens Head, Meriden

After crossing the M6 we can enjoy more of the same undulating agricultural terrain, but with several areas of large woods. We also catch a glimpse of Coventry to the east, just before we enter the woods of Meriden Shafts. The last length of this section follows a

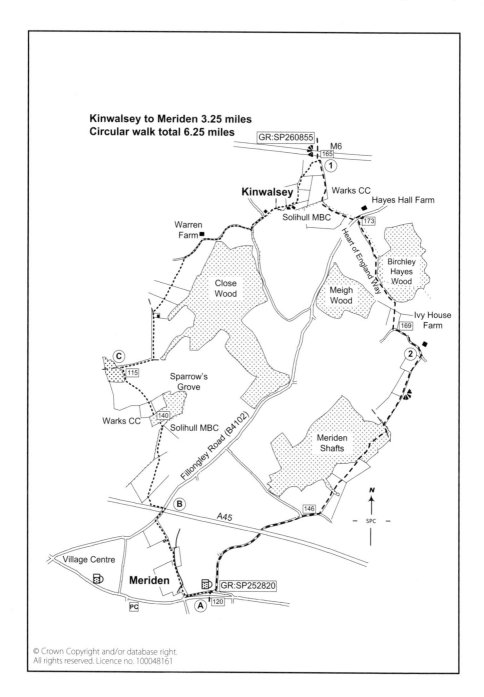

Kinwalsey to Meriden 3.25 miles
Circular walk total 6.25 miles

GR:SP260855

M6

Kinwalsey

Warks CC

Hayes Hall Farm

Solihull MBC

Heart of England Way

Warren Farm

Birchley Hayes Wood

Close Wood

Meigh Wood

Ivy House Farm

C

Sparrow's Grove

Warks CC

Solihull MBC

Fillongley Road (B4102)

Meriden Shafts

B

A45

N

SPC

Village Centre

Meriden

GR:SP252820

PC

A

The village of Meriden

fairly quiet lane under the A45 to reach Meriden, at the Queens Head pub which is close to the ancient centre of the village.

Today the established centre of the village is nearly a mile away, past the village duck pond and the Bulls Head pub, to the village green. There, a Grade II listed monument testifies that Meriden is the centre of England, although today's technologies prove otherwise. Next to it is another obelisk, erected in 1921, in memory of all the cyclists that gave their lives during the First World War.

Our return to the M6 takes us from the old Coventry Road through fields to cross the A45. The footpaths continue through agricultural land and a short length of quiet lane, before crossing some awkward, narrow stiles, erected by the Probation Service, to reach the M6 motorway.

Walk Directions

1. Exit M6 bridge and take the gate on the right and cross the field ½ left. Take the gate, cross the field ¼ right and take the gate. Continue with the left hedge (as we cross the Warwickshire CC to Solihull MBC boundary) take the gate, cross the field and take the stile to a narrow busy road at Hayes Hall Farm. Turn left, cross the road to take the stile and turn right. Continue a few metres to the field corner and turn left to follow the field edge and reach Birchley Hayes Wood. Turn right and continue around the wood perimeter to reach a marker post. Turn right and cross the field, take the bridge

and continue across the field and take the gate and turn left along lane.

2. Just past Ivy House Farm take the stile on the right and follow the left hedge with views to Coventry. Take the stile and at the 2nd gate turn left along the path around the perimeter of Meriden Shafts Wood. After 50m take a gate on the right and follow the path through the wood. Exit the wood via a gate and bridge and continue straight ahead across the field to take a stile. Continue with the left hedge to take a stile and turn right along the lane. After 150m turn left along Eaves Green Lane. Continue for 800m and turn right at the Queens Head Pub to reach the embankment steps on the left in front of the pub.

A. *Pass the steps and continue almost to the junction with the main road, take the gate on the right. Cross the field, go through a hedge gap and cross a bridge. Follow the stream, then ditch, up the hill, turning left and right then pass the pond. Continue through a gap in the hedge and with the right hedge reach and take the gate to Meriden Road. Cross over the road turn right over the A45 and take the gate on the left.*

B. *Follow the path at the top of the cutting and take the gate. Cross the field corner ½ left, take the stile, cross the field ½ right (crops) to take the stile. Cross the field to a gate visible ahead but ignore this gate and turn left to take the gate in the hedge. Follow the footpath, take the gate to go through the wood and exit adjacent a hedge. Continue with the hedge on the right and take the stile. Cross the field ½ left down hill (crops), to the corner of the wood and turn right alongside wood to reach a track.*

C. *Turn right along the track, up hill to reach a gate way and turn left with the left hedge down hill along a track. Adjacent a house go ½ right to a power line pole. Follow the line of the poles (crops) to reach a lane and turn right. Continue up the lane to a junction and turn left along the lane for 150m. At Church Tree Barn turn right along a drive and after 100m take a track on the left. Follow the track for 50m and the take stile on the right. Continue across 2 fields and take 2 stiles. After the 2nd stile turn left and follow the left fence, take the stile and cross the field ½ right to the M6 bridge.*

Chapter 5

Section 14: Meriden to Berkswell

From the Queens Head we cross the Coventry Road and climb through fields to the church of St Laurence, which is of Norman origin, as are most of the churches on the Way. Earliest references to it are as the 'Chapel of Alspath', in 1183. The church was extended in the 13th and 15th centuries with later additions. There are five bells, the oldest of which is from the 14th century, three were cast in 1740 and the fifth in 1890. The views from the church yard extend to beyond Birmingham, south-west to the Clent Hills and north-west to Barr Beacon. You may wish to rest on the Heart of England Way bench erected by our Association and view our interpretation board.

With the proximity of Birmingham and Coventry it is easy to see why this area is known as the Meriden Gap, a gap both conurbations are determined to retain, so that the countryside remains for everyone

Birkswell Church

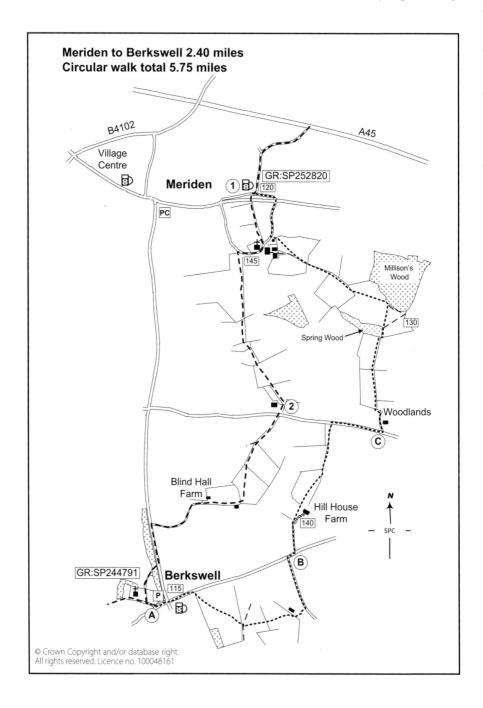

Meriden to Berkswell 2.40 miles
Circular walk total 5.75 miles

B4102

A45

Village Centre

Meriden (1) GR:SP252820 120

PC

145

Millison's Wood

130

Spring Wood

(2)

Woodlands

C

Blind Hall Farm

Hill House Farm
140

N

SPC

B

GR:SP244791 Berkswell

P 115

A

to enjoy. The route to Berkswell is through pleasant, rolling farmland and then a track, at Blind Hall Farm, to the road and this very attractive village.

The village name is probably derived from the Anglo Saxon name Berculswell. The 16 feet deep well still exists today, next to the 12th century church. Berkswell is an ancient site which was held by the Count of Meulan, according to the Domesday Book. The village stocks are probably 200 years old and the five holes, it's reputed, were designed to 'arrest' three persistent offenders one of whom had only one leg but more likely the sixth hole has rotted away.

The church of St John Baptist was built on the site of an earlier Saxon church and its registers date from 1653. Most of the carved woodwork was undertaken by Robert Thompson of Yorkshire. The first piece was the 1926 pulpit and the carvers mark of a mouse can be spotted by the eagle eyed.

The villages most famous resident was Maud Watson (1864-1946), who is buried in the church yard. She won the first ladies Wimbledon Lawn Tennis championships in 1884. Lettice Floyd is also buried in the churchyard. She gained national notoriety as a suffragette serving a month in prison for the suffragette rush on the House of Commons on 13th October, 1908.

Returning to Meriden we pass the Bear Inn in Lavender Hill Lane and once again follow easy footpaths, with a little road work, to reach Meriden close to St Laurence Church.

Walk Directions

1. Take the steps opposite the Old Queens Head and cross over the road and take 2 gates into the field. Follow the left hedge through 2 gates to the churchyard of St Laurence. At a fenced tomb turn left to the road, turn right noting the HoEW Information Board and bench. Continue along the lane for 200m and, at the 2nd bend, take the gate on the left. Cross the field and then continue with the left hedge around a corner to take a plank bridge. Follow the left hedge, take a gate; cross the end of the field ½ left, take the stile and follow the left hedge to take a gate. Continue up the field with the left hedge then ½ left, to take a gate, now cross the field ½ left take a gate and follow a drive to the road.

2. Cross the road, take the stile and follow a track with the hedge on

the left then on the right. As the track turns through the hedge again, leave the track and follow a path left with the hedge on the right. Continue with the hedge to cross a a bridge on the right, take a gate and then go left around the pond. From the pond cross the field towards a house and take the gate on the right. Join a track and continue past Blind Hall Farm to the Meriden Road. Turn left for 300m and before the parking area, cross the road and take a gate. Follow the footpath through the gates to the churchyard and then take a gate to the road. Turn right to continue along the Way.

A. *To return to Meriden turn left, then left along Lavender Hall Lane. Continue across the junction with the Meriden Road, pass the Bear Inn, and just after Pound Close take the footpath on the right and the gate. Cross the field ½ left, take a stile and turn right and left through the hedge gap and cross the field. Take a stile, cross the field to turn right at a gate and follow the left hedge to the corner and take the gate on the left. Follow the footpath, turn right along a drive to reach the lane. Turn left and continue to the junction with the Coventry Road and turn right.*

B. *After 50m take the drive on the left to Hill House Farm. Ignore the right fork to the house and continue to reach and cross the farm yard and take the gate. Cross the field slightly right to take the corner gate. Follow the track, keeping the hedge on the right to reach Back Lane. Turn right for 400m and turn left along the track adjacent Woodland's Farm.*

C. *Follow the track, which eventually drops down across a field to Spring Wood. At a gate to the wood turn right and on the left take the stiles and bridge. Continue with the edge of the wood on the left then across the field to Millison's Wood and turn left (see map if crops obstruct). Follow the edge of wood for a few metres then bear left to cross the field to take a gate in the left hedge and turn right. Continue along the track for 250m and take a gate into an open field with a hedge on the left. Follow the track until it bends left, then go ½ right taking a route established by the farmer, to take a corner gate and at the road turn right. Follow the road to cross the Birmingham Road and turn left along Old Road to the Queens Head.*

Section 15: Berkswell to Temple Balsall

We leave the village alongside the church and follow a raised board walk with a view of Berkswell Hall to our right. On the way to the A452 dual carriageway we re-cross the route of the High Speed Railway and then the present Birmingham – London line. Despite the proximity to the spreading dormitory sprawl of Balsall Common our route follows quiet footpaths around its outskirts. We cross the B4040 and enter Magpie Lane, alongside the 16th century Saracens Head pub, and then cross a field to re-enter the lane opposite the handsome Balsall Common Farmhouse. Up ahead you will see timber framed black and white Magpie Cottage, which you may like to take a closer look at before continuing right across the fields.

This section of the Way terminates at a footpath cross roads, which although not an appropriate place to actually start and finish, provides our halfway point between Berkswell and Baddesley Clinton. To return to Berkswell you turn right along a field edge and, after crossing the road, drop down to follow and cross the River Blythe. This river, although only 39km (24 miles) long, is unique amongst English rivers. From its source, at Spring Brook, its natural head waters are the most southerly that, via the Rivers Tame and Trent, end up in the North Sea and, by virtue of 19th century engineering via a feeder reservoir to the Stratford Canal and the River Avon, also find the Bristol Channel.

The Blythe's entire area, some 252 acres, is a Site of Special Scientific Interest (SSSI) under Section 28 of the Wildlife and Countryside Act. This quiet stream is "a particularly fine example of lowland river on clay". According to the SSSI notification it has a wide range of natural features such as riffles, pools, small cliffs and meanders. I can testify that it even has a small oxbow lake.

The river also has a wide variation in sub-strata types and a succession of differing river features ranging from the tree and shrub lined upper reaches to the faster moving shallower sections, together with the poorly drained, often flooded, adjacent meadows. This diversity means that the number of plant species found in any kilometre stretch is above average for its type, as is the total number recorded for its whole length. Botanically the Blythe is one of the richest in lowland England, containing as many species as the very richest, 'poet lauded', chalk streams.

The river also supports a diverse invertebrate community and, apparently, the most notable species is the pea-shell cockle. There are also dragonflies including, according to the Warwickshire County Council website, the least common, beautiful *Calopterys vigo.*

There you have it. The short, narrow, winding River Blythe can flow along there with the widest and longest.

After crossing the river we enter Barston through the churchyard of St Swithin's. The present church is early 18th century with 'Victorian interruption'. It is believed that there was a church on the site from the 11th century. Next door is the Malt Shovel pub but we turn right from the church passing the impressive Barston Hall, and then following a lane passing Marsh Farm to cross the Blythe at the West Midlands Golf Club. The area is known as Bradnock's Marsh, so I believe winter conditions on the golf course can be rather soft!

After crossing the A452, our path crosses and parallels the route of the proposed High Speed Railway and we return to Berkswell.

Walk Directions

1. Take Church Lane, enter the churchyard of St John the Baptist and follow the path, take 3 gates and continue along the board walk. Cross the bridge and continue along a fenced footpath through the wood. Take a gate straight ahead and follow right hedge through a field to the road and turn right. Follow the road to the A452, turn left for a few metres then cross the dual carriage way. Turn left over the railway line and turn right into Wootton Lane and left into Wootton Green Lane.

2. Follow the lane, then straight ahead along Wooton Grange drive. At the right hand bend, take the stile on the left and turn right to follow the right hedge, turn left at the corner and continue to take the stiles and a bridge. Follow the right hedge to the summit of a field then cross the field ¼ left to take a stile. Continue straight ahead across the field via a bridge and take a stile. Follow the right hedge and take 2 stiles to reach the B4101. Turn left along the road to the Old Saracens Head and turn right into Magpie Lane.

3. Continue around the bend in the lane and take a gate on the right. Cross the field ½ left and take the corner gate. Turn left along lane for 100m, take the stile on the right. Follow the right hedge, around a pool then straight ahead to cross to the bottom of the field. Take the bridge

and stile and cross the field ½ left, take a stile and cross the field along the line of remaining hedge and take the stile. Continue with the hedge on the left under a power line to a double stile. To continue along the Heart of England Way take stile and turn left.

A. *To return to Berkswell take the second stile and turn right, follow the right hedge around the field, take a stile to the B4101. Turn left along the road for 90m and take the stile on the right, sign posted 'Barston'. Cross the field ½ right, down the slope, around the 'bowl', turning ¼ right to follow the contour to the River Blythe. Follow the river and cross at the bridge. Cross the field ½ right, through a hedge gap, and follow hedge on the left to take the gate in the corner. Turn left then right, take the gate into the churchyard of St Swithin's and continue through to reach the road, near to the Bulls Head.*

B. *Turn right, continue along the road and just after Barston Hall turn left along the farm access road 'Ryton End'. Take the gate, enter the golf course and follow the track as it turns to the river. Continue along the line of the river to reach the golf course access drive. Turn right over the bridge and continue along the lane then alongside the railway before turning left into Bradnock's Marsh Lane. Continue under the bridge to the roundabout at the A452.*

C. *Turn left in front of the car dealership and cross the dual carriage way turn left and before the speed camera, take the gate on the right. Go through the plantation, take the gate and follow the right hedge to take a gate and turn right. Follow the right hedge and take a stile and follow the path around the edge of the wood. After a pond take a gate and turn left around the field edge to take a gate. Continue with the hedge on the left, then through a wood and take a gate. Follow the well marked path across the field to return to the HoEW, turn left over the bridge and the follow board walk to return to Berkswell.*

Section 16: Temple Balsall to Baddesley Clinton

From the footpath crossroads we now follow a totally rural series of footpaths, follow a long re-entrant containing a series of streams, which emerge from springs just below the southerly edge of the midland plateau. After we cross Oldwich Lane, and turn south-west, 500m south-east is the runway of an old RAF base.

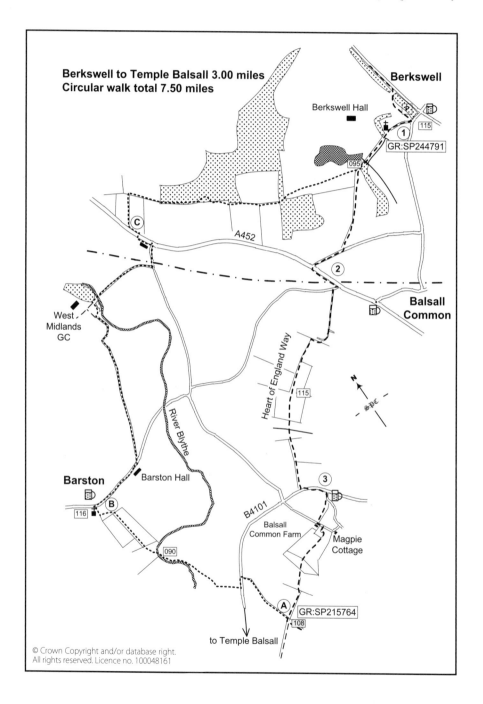

Berkswell to Temple Balsall 3.00 miles
Circular walk total 7.50 miles

Berkswell

Berkswell Hall

115

GR:SP244791

095

C

A452

2

Balsall
Common

West
Midlands
GC

Heart of England Way

115

N

River Blythe

Barston

Barston Hall

116

B

090

3

B4101

Balsall
Common Farm

Magpie
Cottage

A

GR:SP215764

108

to Temple Balsall

Back in 1941, for the airmen of RAF Honiley, taking off south-west, from the edge of the plateau, it must have been an exhilarating experience as they headed over the Avon valley between Alcester and Stratford-upon-Avon. Circuits and bumps exercises would have given them the distraction of a bird's eye view of both Warwick and Kenilworth Castles.

The base, which closed in 1957, was originally built as a training station but its strategic position, to the south of Birmingham and Coventry, meant that it was soon converted to a night fighter base. 605 (County of Warwick) Squadron, Royal Auxiliary Air Force, which was formed in 1926, were based here at the end of 1941. Prior to then, equipped with Hurricanes, they fought on the front line at Dunkirk, and in the Battle of Britain.

At the end of 1941, 605 were shipped to the Far East and some flying elements were landed to defend Malta but, by March 1942 the squadron ceased to exist. Later, in 1942, the Squadron was reformed, fighting until the end of the war, during which time 148 of its men had given their lives. After 605's departure from Honiley the station settled into its role of night interdiction and over the next two years a number of squadrons rotated through there. In 1943, with German aggression over England diminished, the station's role was reduced to training and storage.

After the war, in 1946, Honiley was re-activated, hosting a reformed part time Royal Auxiliary Air Force 605 Squadron. In 1948 they became the first Auxiliary squadron to fly jet fighters, when they converted to Vampires and were also joined by a Royal Naval Volunteer Reserve Squadron flying Sea Vampires. The local residents must have certainly 'enjoyed' some fairly noisy weekends and rambling through the area must have also been diverting. In March 1957, the cost and difficulties of training part time personnel in the operation of such complicated aircraft, brought to an end the era of flying reserve squadrons and the closure of Honiley. Today you may still enjoy an air display as a procession of aircraft make their final approaches to Birmingham Airport.

We continue to Chadwick End where, as we cross the Birmingham Road, we also cross the Trent and Avon watershed. From the village the Way provides the only path to Baddesley Clinton. You may choose to return to Temple Balsall from adjacent the Orange Tree pub, if you do not wish to walk the same path twice.

The path along the Way from Chadwick End crosses a board walk erected by Association volunteers and then we cross fields and go through a stable yard. We then follow the drive passing the Poor Clares Convent. This site had been originally a Franciscan Order founded in 1793 but the present house was built in 1870 for the Poor Clares, who arrived from Bruges, to re-establish their order for the first time since the Reformation.

Baddesley Clinton Manor

A long footpath approaches Baddesley Clinton and the Way crosses the drive to the house. This family house, dating from the 15th century, was the home of the Ferrers family for 500 years and passed to the National Trust in 1980. The house and interiors are Elizabethan reflecting the period of its heyday. Then it was a haven for persecuted Catholics who could be hidden in the three priest's holes. The house and gardens are well worth a visit. Just up the lane, on the return path of the next section, the quaint church of St. Michael's, shares much of its history with the house.

Our walk back retraces our steps to Chadwick End where, after crossing the road, a short path across a field leads us to a quiet lane passing the impressive Chadwick Manor, whose manorial residents now occupy luxurious apartments. At end of the lane we take a field path and approach Temple Balsall, which is screened by trees, so there is no anticipation of this impressive site.

In the reign of King Stephen (1097-1154) the manor of Temple Balsall was granted to the Order of Knights Templar. The order, founded in 1118 to fulfil the dual role of monk and knight, built the first church. They organised village life until their dissolution in 1324. The manor was taken over by the Knights of St John of Jerusalem, and when they in turn were dissolved the manor passed to the crown. The ownership passed to the Earl of Leicester's family and his grand-daughter, Lady Katharine Leveson, who re-established the original owners' good works.

On her death in 1674 she willed that a charity be established to provide a hospital building next to the church, for twenty poor widows, and a free school for twenty poor boys. Provision was also made for a minister to the church, who would also be the Master of the hospital and teach the boys.

The old hall occupied by the Knights Templar, which predates the church, although rebuilt, still retains its original 12th century timber frame. The Almshouses and the Master's House were replaced by new buildings in the early 18th and 19th centuries respectively.

Temple Balsall – The Chapel of the Knights Templar

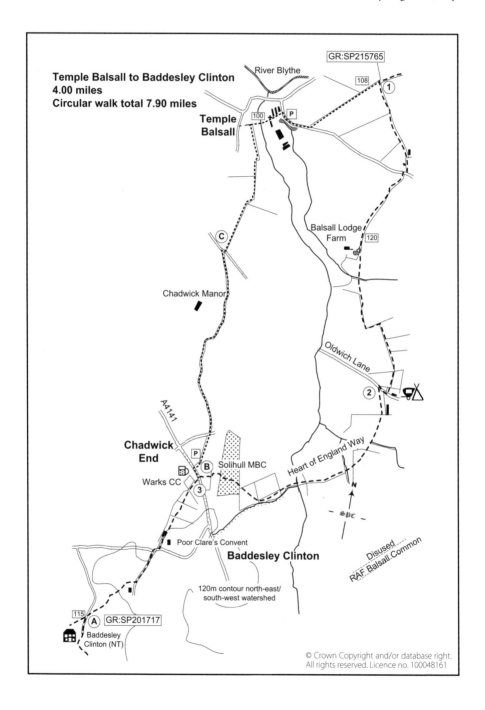

Walk Directions

1. From the double stile follow the left hedge take a stile, continue to the farm buildings and follow a path between hedges to the road. Turn right and then left along concrete drive signed Balsall Lodge Farm. Continue to the right hand bend at the approach to the farm buildings and take the track on the left. Continue downhill, passing a pond on the right, and cross the field to take a gap in the hedge left of a tree. Cross the field, to a hedge corner and follow the hedge on the right through a copse. Continue now with the hedge on the left, take a stile, turn left pass an old wall, take a stile, turn right and follow the right hedge, taking 2 stiles. At a gated fence intersection, turn right and left to continue with the fence on the left. Reach a power pole, take a stile, follow the right hedge, take a gate and continue a few metres to Oldwich Lane.

2. Turn right and take the stile on the left. Turn ½ left, pass the houses and take a stile in the hedge. Cross the field ½ right, pass a power pole, cross a bridge, continue across the field and take a stile. Cross the field ½ right and through a gap in the hedge. Follow the left hedge, take a gate and continue around the field to take a stile. Continue with the left fence and take a bridge. Go straight on through a gap and now with the fence on the right continue to take a gate. Cross the field ½ right to take a gate, left of a barn. Cross a track and take a stile, turn right, left and right and follow the path through the wood. Exit the wood and follow the left hedge to take the gate and path left, at the rear of the houses. Turn right, pass the garages and then left along the drive way to the A4141. .

3. Turn left for a few metres and cross the road to take the gate. Follow the right hedge along a board walk and take the gate. Follow the left hedge and take 4 stiles through the fields, then through a yard take a stile to a drive and follow it to a road. Turn right then left along lane to Hay Wood and after 300m, just before Bromes Park, take a gate on the right and follow the fenced path to the drive of Baddesley Clinton.

A. *To return to the start retrace the route to Chadwick End via the fenced footpath to Hay Wood Lane. Turn left along the lane, then right at the junction and take the drive to Convent Farm. Take the stile through yard and stile into field. Continue with hedge on right through fields, take 4 stiles then follow left hedge, boardwalk and take the stile to the road. .*

B. *Cross the A4141, turn left until opposite the Orange Tree Pub and take the footpath on the right, behind the bungalows. Continue with the hedge on the left to reach Oldwich Lane West. Turn right and left into the pleasant and quiet Chadwick Lane and continue to Old Green Lane and turn right.*

C. *After 25m take the stile on the left and follow the right hedge around 2 large fields to reach the 2nd power pole and turn left. Follow the right hedge and after the 2nd gate turn right along a surfaced path passing St Mary's Church and the Lady Katherine Homes and school. Turn left to the car park and take the path right, parallel with the road. Rejoin the road for 100m and take a gate on the left and follow the left hedge to reach a stile and the Heart of England Way.*

Chapter 6

Section 17: Baddesley Clinton to Lowsonford

From Baddesley Clinton the Heart of England Way has two alternative routes to reach Lowsonford. I have chosen the western arm as our route south, which crosses fields and soon reaches Kingswood. Here we join the 137 mile long Grand Union Canal, linking Birmingham and London, and next to it is the Navigation pub. This section of the canal between Birmingham and Warwick, was opened in 1844.

A short distance along the canal we cross a bridge and take the arm which links it to the Stratford-upon-Avon canal. This canal, opened in 1816, is first generation, avoiding the engineering feats of later canals as it contours through the countryside from Kings Norton to Stratford-upon-Avon. The canal was built by local entrepreneurs' intent of ensuring that Stratford's historic position as a market centre was not by-passed by this new, revolutionary form of transport. Investors felt their money would be safe as connecting the canal to River Avon would also provide the link between Birmingham and Bristol.

Unfortunately the Birmingham and Worcester canal proved a much quicker route, and with the River Avon not being made navigable, the section south of Lapworth was not successful. The arrival of the railways hastened its decline and, in 1846, it was purchased by a railway company, who in turn were taken over by Great Western Railway in 1863. Despite the new owners, the canal proved to have no real practical use and, in 1950, Warwickshire County Council gave notice of their intention to close it as it had not been used commercially for 3 years.

However, all was not lost. In the face of the threat of closure of many canals, following their nationalisation, dedicated enthusiasts founded the Inland Waterways Association. A Midlands Branch was established, lead by David Hutchings, and the Stratford-upon-Avon Canal Society was formed to try to save the canal. They bought a toll ticket and paddling, dragging and carrying a large canoe they inspected the section from Stratford to Lapworth and confirmed its dire state.

However their adventure proved to be the undoing of Warwickshire County Council's notice of closure. The toll ticket proved that the canal had been used commercially and, against a lot of political resentment, the Society started the campaign to reopen the canal. Eventually, after much persuasion, the National Trust decided to buy the canal and appointed David Hutchings as Manager with the job of repairing it. Its metamorphosis began with a fund of £42,000 from well-wishers and charities, augmented through David Hutchings' subsequent legendary battles with local authorities for more cash.

In a pioneering move, he recruited teams of prisoners from Birmingham's Winson Green prison to help with lock building. There were also many other voluntary workers, including army units. Finally the work was completed and, in 1964, the Queen opened the renovated canal. Although the canal was operated by the National Trust for a number of years, it never really fitted with the rest of their operations and returned to the national canal network ownership and British Waterways.

The indefatigable David Hutchings work was not yet finished. After taking a few years break, he was persuaded to join the Upper Avon Navigation Trust. The river between Stratford and Evesham had

Lock Keepers Cottage

ceased to be fully navigable in the 1870s and so, as project manager, he began the battle to reopen it. Five years on the Queen Mother re-opened the restored river and later David Hutchings was awarded the MBE for his sterling service. The work provided the missing link in a 110-mile waterway circle joining Birmingham, Stourport, Tewkesbury and Stratford.

The canal with its unique, barrel-roved, lock keepers cottages is picturesque and quiet, except where it crosses under the M40. Just before we reach Lowsonford we walk under the disused bridge of the old railway line linking the Great Western's London and Bristol lines. We reach Lowsonford close to the canal side Fleur de Lys Pub, famed for its meat pies.

To return to Baddesley Clinton from the canal, we turn left along the lane, crossing the M40 and railway to make our way across fields and the Grand Union Canal to Rowington. After crossing the road we make our way through the church yard of St Laurence, with its impressive tower holding six bells, the oldest dated 1609. Our return to Baddesley Clinton is mostly pleasant field paths and tracks, but the length of lane takes us past the only surviving windmill 'Bouncing Bess' in Rowington Green, now converted into a house.

Walk Directions

This section of the Heart of England Way has two alternative routes and therefore the circular route gives the opportunity to walk both of them.

1. At the fork in the drive to Baddesley Clinton take the gate on the right and cross the field ½ right, then follow the fence on the left to take a gate. Cross the culverted stream and continue with the left fence to take a gate. Cross the field ½ right following the sweeping pathway, to the left corner of the barn. Take the gate and follow the drive, take a stile, and continue to join the Old Warwick Road B4439. Turn right and pass the Navigation pub. Cross the bridge over the Grand Union Canal and then cross the road to take the steps down to the tow path.

2. Follow the tow path for 300m, cross the bridge and turn right along the link arm tow path. Cross the bridge right, continue around the house and take the bridge over the Stratford-upon-Avon Canal. Turn left and follow the tow path towards Stratford. The 2.8km

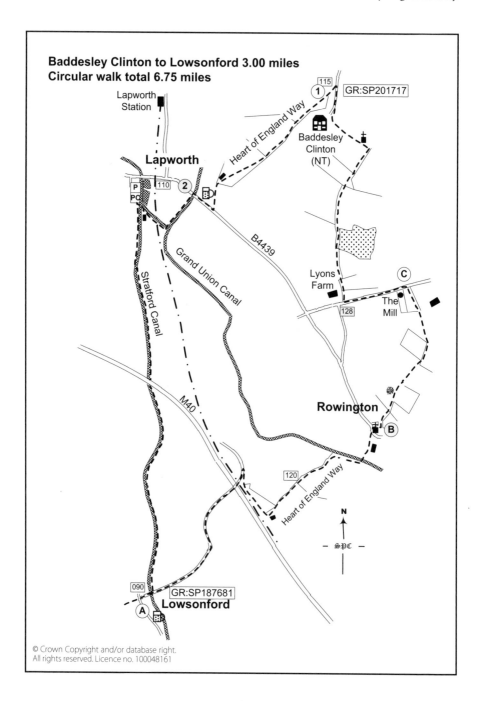

Baddesley Clinton to Lowsonford 3.00 miles
Circular walk total 6.75 miles

Lapworth Station

GR:SP201717

Heart of England Way

Baddesley Clinton (NT)

Lapworth

P
PO

B4439

Grand Union Canal

Stratford Canal

Lyons Farm

C

The Mill

M40

Rowington

B

Heart of England Way

N

SPC

GR:SP187681

Lowsonford

A

walk along the winding towpath, to reach Lowsonford, is very pleasant, except for the short section disturbed by the adjacent M40. Reaching the bridge at Lowsonford join the road and turn right to the T-junction or return to Baddesley Clinton.

A. *From the bridge turn left and follow the road for 1200m. Cross the M40 and the Birmingham – London railway line and take the concrete drive on the right. Follow the drive up the hill to the communications building and turn left. Continue with the left hedge through 2 fields to turn right with the hedge and join a track turning left over the Grand Union Canal. Continue along the track and take the gate to the B4439, cross the road and enter St Laurence churchyard.*

B. *Go to the left of the church, pass a locked WC and take the stile. Continue with the 'Ha Ha' on your left, to take a stile and turn right. Follow the right hedge, cross a ditch and take a stile. Continue with the hedge, then straight ahead, along the line of trees, to take a stile. Cross the field, take a gate and follow the left hedge to the corner. Cross the field ½ left, take the gate to the left of the farm gate by the power line. Follow the right hedge to take a gate to the lane.*

C. *Turn left along the lane for 450m and take a gate on the right marked 'bridleway' adjacent Lyons Farm. Continue along the track, pass the barns, take the gates and, just after the coppice, keep straight ahead and take the gate. Follow the left hedge, take a gate, cross the bridge, then bear left to follow the right hedge and take the gate. Continue along the fenced path to join a drive and turn left to reach St Michaels Church. Continue through the church yard and then along the path to reach Baddesley Clinton. Turn right along the drive.*

Section 18: Lowsonford to Henley-in-Arden

From Lowsonford we climb and turn right between two brick walls, which formed the bridge over the now filled in railway line. The undulating paths lead us to an escarpment face and the climb over the Mount and descent to Henley-in-Arden. Although its name evokes gentility, major expansion in the twentieth century has robbed Henley of being regarded as a quintessential rural idyll. Nevertheless it has eschewed the need to attract industry and therefore retains a sense of history.

The Mount, over which we scrambled, although probably an Ancient Briton hill fort, was also the site of the Norman stone and timber castle. In the late 12th century Thurstan de Montfort was granted the title of the Manor of Beaudesert. He also built the church of St Nicholas at the bottom of the Mount. The church is noted for its beautiful Norman arches, and the east window is virtually untouched and is reputed to be one of the finest windows of its type in the county.

St Nicholas Church Norman entrance

As we cross the River Alne we enter the historically separate parish of Henley-in-Arden. Its development was due to Thurstan's successor, Peter, being granted a charter to hold a weekly fair and market. The successes of this venture lead to the traders and users of the market establishing their homes and the beginning of the village. Unfortunately there was a setback for, in 1220, Peter de Montfort fought against the King at the Battle of Evesham and lost. Not surprisingly retribution was sought and his castle was demolished and Henley put to the torch. But Henley's market continued and, by the time of the 14th century's Black Death and famines, it had established itself well enough to retain its status as a trading centre. A walk along the High Street reveals that, because of its longevity, Henley has examples of buildings from most periods from the Middle Ages onward.

Eventually, in 1367, the people of Henley were given permission to establish their own chapel, and thus saved them the arduous journey to their own parish church at Wootton Wawen. In 1448 the present church was built and it housed the Chapel of the Guild of St John. In 1546 Henry VIII confiscated the church because of its connections with the guild. However Edward VI was persuaded to return it to the worthy parishioners of Henley.

Henley in Arden High Street

Henley thus remained a fairly static centre, eventually having its road connecting Birmingham and Stratford turned into a turnpike in 1725. In 1836 a coach route was established, which brought a new source of employment to the town and a number inns and taverns. The railway came to Henley in 1894, when the now removed branch was opened in 1894. The main North Warwickshire line, which exists today, opened in 1908, although it terminates at Stratford-upon-Avon.

Our return route goes east from Henley and climbs through fields to Preston Bagot. Passing Church Farm and then taking the path, beside the entrance to the Old Rectory bed and breakfast, we climb the hill to the fascinating 'cottage' Church of All Saints. The nave is 12th century and the chancel was probably added in the 15th century. Later additions and alterations were made, including the bell tower with its two bells and its five 19th century Burne-Jones windows.

From the church we continue along the lane which continues into a bridleway to cross the Preston Bagot Brook and return to Lowsonford.

Walk Directions

1. From the canal bridge go to the T-junction, cross straight over and take the surfaced drive. Adjacent a cottage take the stile on the right into the field and follow the hedge on the right and then continue across the field to take a stile and continue to take the next stile. Turn right over the old railway bridge, then turn left through 2 gates and follow the hedge on the left to enter the wood. Follow the wide path through the wood, then right along the edge of the wood, to take a gate on the left. Cross the field to a double gate, turn right, follow the left hedge, and take a gate to a drive. Turn left to reach the road and turn right.

2. Cross a bridge and take the pedestrian gate on the right. Go ½ left, cross the drive to the house, and take a gap in the hedge. Continue with the hedge on the right, pass a hedge on the left and cross field ½ left, towards 2 trees. Continue with the hedge on the left and take the corner gate. Cross the field ½ left, go through the coppice and take the gate. Cross the field ½ left to a hedge corner, follow the right hedge, through a gap in the hedge, cross the drive and

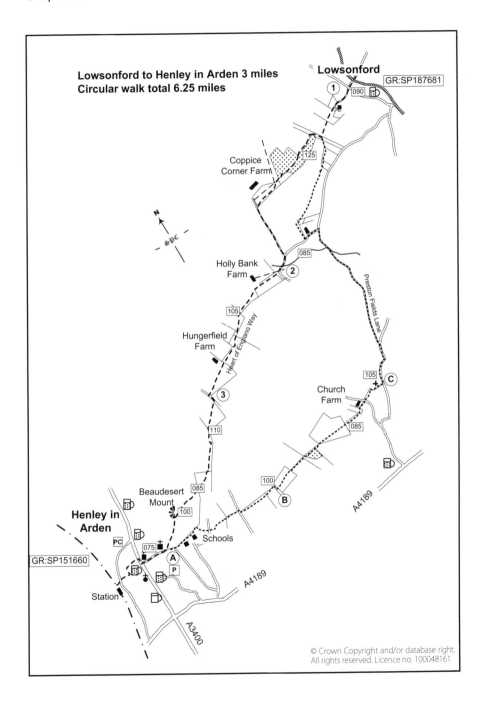

Lowsonford to Henley in Arden 3 miles
Circular walk total 6.25 miles

Lowsonford
GR:SP187681
1   090

Coppice
Corner Farm   125

N

Holly Bank
Farm   085
2

105
Hungerfield
Farm

Heart of England Way

Preston Fields Lane

Church   105   C
Farm

3

085

110

Beaudesert   085
Mount   100
Henley in
Arden
PC   075
GR:SP151660   A
P
Station

Schools
100   B
A4189

A4189

A3400

continue across the field to a wooded path. Turn left along the path and take a stile on the right.

3. Cross the field ½ left, take a corner stile and turn ½ left to follow the steep, scarp edge. Continue straight ahead under the power line and descend the slope, following the path to ascend the undulating, Mount. Enjoy the views all along this section of Henley and the distant Bannam's Wood. Descend the steep hill and take the gate, adjacent the Church of St Nicholas. Turn right to continue along the Way and follow Beaudesert Lane to the High Street: or turn left to return to Lowsonford

A. *From the gate turn left and follow the public footpath between the Mount and school grounds. Continue between the houses, crossing the road and take the gate to a park. Continue ½ left and climb the steps. At the top, take a stile turn right, take the next stile turn left and continue with the left hedge to take a stile to the road. Cross the road slightly right and take the stile. Continue with the left hedge taking 2 stiles, then a gate, cross a ditch and take another stile and turn right along wooded path.*

B. *After 25m take a stile on the left and cross straight over the field and take a stile. Continue straight ahead and take a stile and enter a plantation. Continue with the left hedge through 2 gates and cross the field ¼ right and take a gate. Continue with the left hedge, taking 3 gates, adjacent to Church Farm to reach the lane. Cross the lane and take a gate and footpath leading, via a gate, to All Saints Church. Continue along the path, pass the church on the left, to reach Rookery Lane and turn left.*

C. *Continue along lane for 300m and turn left into Preston Fields Lane. Continue as the lane becomes a rutted 'Unclassified County Road', crossing the stream via a concrete plank bridge. At end of the lane turn left along Preston Road for 150m and take the stile on the right. Follow the right hedge, take a stile and turn ½ left, take a stile, turn ½ right and cross the field via a marker post. Take a stile and follow the path, take a stile and steps then turn left and re-join HoEW taking the stile on the right to return to Lowsonford.*

Chapter 7

Section 19: Henley-in-Arden to Bannam's Wood

Between Henley and Alcester there is no parking opportunity except in Great Alne, in the lane adjacent to Coughton Court and on a wide verge, where the return path to Alcester meets Spernal Lane.

As we leave Henley-in-Arden, I should note that 'Arden' refers to the historical Forest of Arden, and Henley was considered the capital of the area. In roman times the forest extended from Watling Street in the north, south to the 'Salt Way', the road between Alcester and Stratford, and from Ryknield Street in the West to the Fosse Way in the east. Shakespeare is reputed to have based his play *As You Like It* in the Forest of Arden, which would have been more extensive in his time than today. Perhaps in Bannam's Wood we can capture Shakespeare's allusions of magical places where strange coincidences occur, or where people are transformed through self discovery or by finding love! Certainly on a clear day the walk and climb to the summit in the wood will be rewarded by the rural, Warwickshire vista.

Today another poet is leaving his mark on the landscape, in the form of Felix Dennis who owns Bannam's Wood and some other large estates through which the Way passes. Felix Dennis has definitely made good since, as the co-director of Oz Magazine, he was briefly imprisoned in the 1960s for publishing obscene material, before being released on appeal. Since then, through his magazine publishing empire, he has amassed, in 2011, £500m making him the 10th richest Midlander.

But, as well as being a writer, Felix is determined, through his charitable trust, to re-establish a real broad leaf forest. Planting trees, he says on his web site, does no harm whilst they give enjoyment and are good for our mental health. He has determined that, after hundreds of years of talk about planting trees, he is doing something about it. The ultimate size of the Felix's forest, now named the Heart of England Forest, will depend on how much money he makes, although he has 50,000 acres in mind. He doesn't think he will succeed, but intimates that the project will continue beyond his lifetime.

Since he started his project in the late 1990s by the end of 2011, 1874 acres of new, native broad leaved, woods have been established with plans to progress at the annual rate of 300 acres, which is 1000 trees per year. There will be a number of opportunities to see the evidence of the spreading forest, both on the Way and along the circular routes between here and Dorsington, and for more up to date information you can visit his web site (www.felixdennis.com).

As we exit Bannam's Wood, perhaps after resting on the Heart of England Way bench, kindly donated by Felix Dennis, we enter a narrow lane. The return path to Henley is an equally enjoyable walk through the Forest of Arden.

Walk Directions

1. Commence in 'High Street', the A3400, and take the footpath to the right of the White Swan. Continue via the car park and footpath to the railway station. Cross the railway via the footbridge and continue, past the allotments on the left, then, with the right field edge, through 2 gates to the field corner. Turn left through a gate and continue around the edge of the field to take a bridge on the right. Continue straight ahead between the hedges and take a stile. Climb the bank and turn right with the hedge and then continue across the field and take a stile and then two further stiles to reach the road.

2. Cross the road, through a brick-wall stile, then straight ahead take 2 stiles through a paddock into a field. Continue straight ahead, take a stile, then cross the field ½ left and take a stile into a copse. Take the steps, take a stile then a bridge into the field. Turn ½ left through 3 fields and after the 3rd stile reach a bench. Turn ½ right and cross the field, take a stile and a bridge and continue across the field, to take a stile. Bear right across the field, then follow the right hedge and take the stile and continue to the lane.

3. Cross the lane and take a gate through a copse to follow the right hedge and climb to Bannam's Wood. At the summit follow the path on the right, through a gap in the hedge. Continue as the path winds through the ancient wood land to a sign to a bench from where the view may be admired. Returning to the path continue down through the wood along a winding track passing the HoEW 25th Anniversary bench, provided by Felix Dennis. Take the gate to the lane, turn left and continue to the right hand bend where the route along the Way may be continued or the return to Henley-in-Arden taken.

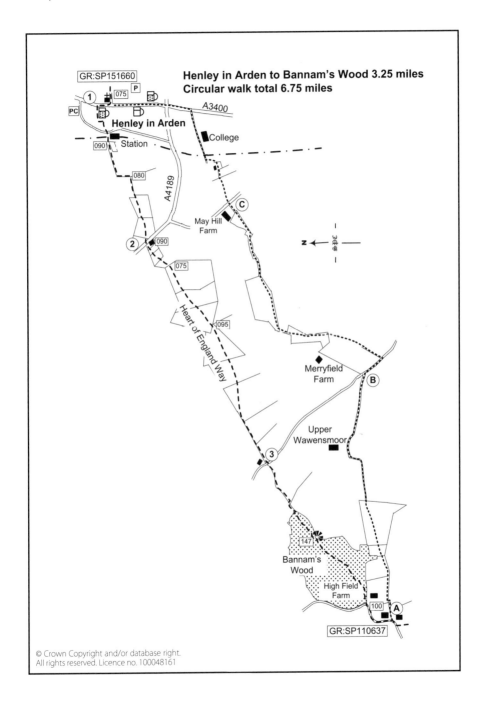

GR:SP151660

**Henley in Arden to Bannam's Wood 3.25 miles
Circular walk total 6.75 miles**

A3400

Henley in Arden

College

Station

May Hill
Farm

Heart of England Way

Merryfield
Farm

Upper
Wawensmoor

Bannam's
Wood

High Field
Farm

GR:SP110637

A. *Just before the bend take the gate on the left marked 'bridleway' and keep to the left fence to reach and take the 2nd gate on the left. Turn right to continue with the right hedge and take 2 gates. Now cross the field and take a gate and continue in the same direction across a large field to take a gate and join a green track. Follow the track as it bends left and right and turn right along the surfaced drive at 'Upper Wawensmoor Farm'. Follow the drive then lane to a road junction and turn right.*

B. *Follow the lane for 150m take the left farm track through a barrier and continue for 450m to take a gate into a field. Follow the hedge on the right and then bear left to take a gate in the field corner. Follow the footpath, take a gate and continue with the right hedge around the field and take a gate. Follow the track, pass a barn and through a gate into an open field with a large barn. Continue around the field following the right fence, take 2 gates, adjacent the farmhouse, and then take a stile to the road.*

C. *Cross the road, take a stile, follow the line of trees across the field and take a gate. Follow the footpath, take a stile, pass a barn, take a gate turn ½ left and, take a gate to a drive. Turn right and follow the drive to the A3400. Turn left and return to Henley-in-Arden.*

Section 20: Bannam's Wood to Spernal Lane

The Way soon leaves the lane and we wind through the quiet countryside, passing the woods of Spernal Park and, on the approach to Alne Wood, the earliest evidence of the new Felix Dennis, Heart of England Forest. The Way continues to, and crosses, Spernal Lane, but our circular walk branches off just before the lane.

Our route takes us to Great Alne's St Mary Magdalene Church. The church, although of 13th century origins, was much enlarged in the 19th century and some roadside parking is possible adjacent to the church. The nearby Mother Huff Cap pub is the only pub on the route between Henley and Alcester. Its' 2010 'gastro pub' make over has possibly put it back on the map. For back in 1675, travellers regarded it as; 'one of the six prime post ways on the London to Shrewsbury road'. Yes, although difficult to imagine in the 17th century, the road through the village was their M6 equivalent .

Maudslay Motor Company, who produced heavy lorries, moved

here during the Second World War, from Coventry. The old manor house was demolished and as we walk along Park Lane we can see their industrial buildings through the trees. The company merged with AEC in 1948 and with the demise of our motor industry the buildings remain as evidence of our recent industrial history. After this interesting diversion, we return to Bannam's Wood and you may possibly regard this experience as the quintessential country walk that, 'you only shared with the wildlife'.

Walk Directions

1. Just beyond the right hand bend take the gate on the left. Cross the field ½ right down hill, to take the gate and bridge. Climb straight ahead through the wood, take a gate and continue with the left hedge, taking a gate, then straight ahead across the field. Take the gate at the corner of the wood and turn left with the hedge, to take a gate. Continue with the left hedge through 3 further gates, to join a lane adjacent a cottage.

2. Turn right along lane for 50m and take the gate on the left. Follow the right hedge and then straight on across the field, to take a gate in the corner. Turn ½ right, (the touching point of the return route), and continue through a plantation, along the right side of a wood. Join and follow a track through the wood. Take a gate, leave the wood, take a further gate at a barn conversion and follow the track to a lane.

3. At the lane turn left for 400m and take the gate on the right at Dinglewell Cottage. Follow the left fence, take a gate and continue down through the field to take a gate. Turn right along the track (passing a gate on the left for the circular return route) to meet Spernal Lane.

A. *Take the gate on the left and cross the field following the ditch to a bridge. Cross the bridge, turn right and continue with the stream on the right, take a gate at a track then take the gate to an 'unclassified road'. Turn left for 250m to take a gate on the right and the footpath across the field to the church of St Mary Magdalene. Continue through the churchyard to the road. Turn left along the road, then left into Park Lane and after 550m, take the gate on the right. Follow the fence*

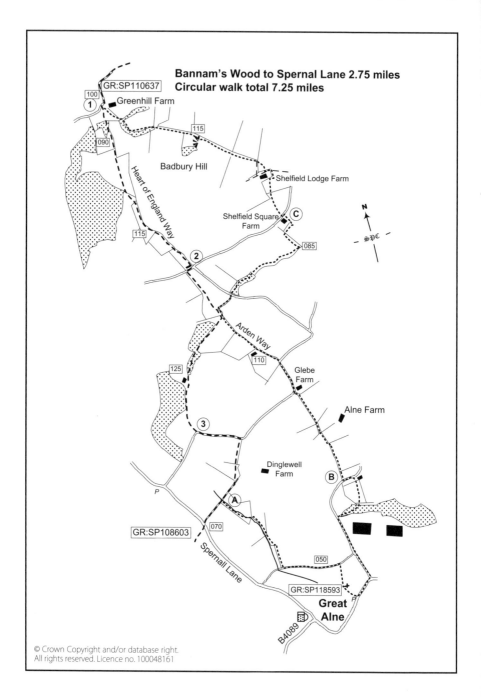

Bannam's Wood to Spernal Lane 2.75 miles
Circular walk total 7.25 miles

GR:SP110637
Greenhill Farm

Badbury Hill

Shelfield Lodge Farm

Shelfield Square Farm

Heart of England Way

Arden Way

Glebe Farm

Alne Farm

Dinglewell Farm

Spernall Lane

GR:SP108603

GR:SP118593

Great Alne

B4089

on the right and through the wood, take the steps and follow the path left and climb to take a gate, leaving the wood. Climb the bank opposite, take a gate and cross the field to take a gate to the left of a large house. Continue to the drive and turn left down hill and after 100m take the steps and gate on the right.

B. *Continue with the fence on the left and at the 2nd gate turn left and right to continue with the fence on the right. Take a gate continue straight ahead along a green ride then follow the left hedge to the road. Turn right and follow the 'Arden Way' and at a bend take the track on the left. Adjacent a large barn take the gate on the left and continue straight ahead with the right hedge. Take a gate but before the next gate (junction of the "Ways") take the track on the right, between the hedges, to a road. Cross the road and follow a path through the wood, cross a plank bridge and continue parallel with the stream and along a field edge to the corner and turn left. Follow the right hedge and at a fence take the gate on the right over a plank bridge. Cross the field with the fence on the left, take the gate, turn left and follow the green ride to the road.*

C. *At the road turn left and right and take the path across the field to the hedge corner. Continue right, over a plank bridge, take a gate to cross the field ½ right to a fence corner. Turn left and follow the fence to a drive. Turn left and right and take a gap in the hedge, cross the field ½ left through gap in the hedge and follow a track straight ahead alongside a new plantation. Continue for 900m over the summit until just ahead of a cross field hedge turn right and left through a hedge gap and continue with the stream/hedge on the left. Ignore a bridge continue to a corner turn left and right with the stream and take a gate. Follow the green hollow way up the field to take the gate to the road.*

Section 21: Spernal Lane to Alcester

The onward walk along the Way soon takes us to Alcester and, after a march along the urban approaches, we find ourselves in its attractive medieval centre.

The High Street is dotted with a mixture of buildings including black and white tudor cottages and Georgian brick town houses and an assortment of pubs and cafes. Perhaps the two most notable

Butter Street, Alcester

buildings are St Nicholas Church, with its 14th century origins, and
the 17th century Town Hall. This building, built in 1618, started its life
as an open arched roofed market hall for farmers to sell their corn,
but in 1641 the upper storey was added. It is also suspected that a
Roman Fort existed on Primrose Hill, over which we walk on our route
south along the Way. Excavations under parts of modern Alcester have
also revealed the remains of 2nd century buildings. To the west of
Ryknild Street evidence has been found of a Roman cemetery, where
over 100 burials have been discovered. Alcester must have been an
important Roman town and it also worth popping into the free History
Museum, open Thursday to Sunday, to find out more about Alcester.

The circular walk north from Alcester follows the Way back to the
River Arrow. The river rises on the eastern slopes of the Lickey Hills,
just outside Birmingham. We follow the river through urban park and
then farmland to Coughton Court. Coughton (pronounced 'coaton')
Court is a National Trust property and one of England's finest Tudor
Houses.

The house has been the home of the Throckmorton Family since
1409. The manor of Coughton has existed since Anglo Saxon times

and its name suggests a settlement or farm known for hunting of woodcock or game birds. The Throckmorton's were fervently Catholic and fervent participators in religious and political intrigue. Two of the nephews were ringleaders in the 1605 Gun Powder Plot to blow up Parliament.

From the ford at Coughton we follow the 'Arden Way', our other long distance footpath. The route is along a 'County Road' which, although unsurfaced, is open to all traffic, so we may find ourselves sharing the 'road' with an occasional 4x4 or off-road motor bike. The road takes us over Windmill Hill with excellent views of the landscape and plenty of opportunity to see more of the expanding Heart of England Forest. At Spernal Lane there is a wide verge on which you may wish to park.

Walk Directions

1. Cross Spernal Lane and take the gate on the right through the hedge. Bear left to take a plank-bridge, pass by a cottage and take a gate on the left and turn right. Follow the hedge for 400m and at a marker post turn right and left through the hedge. Follow the hedge and wood on the left, then through the wood, cross a track

Coughton Court

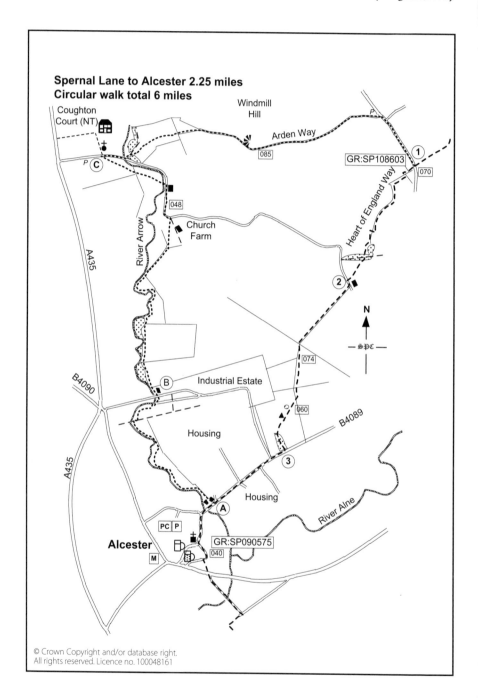

Spernal Lane to Alcester 2.25 miles
Circular walk total 6 miles

and take a gate. Continue ½ right, across the field and take a gate to the lane and turn left for 20m.

2. Take the gate on the right, adjacent a barn, and continue with the hedge on the left climbing the hill for 500m, and then cross through the hedge gap on the left. Continue with the hedge on the right to cross an abandoned railway bridge and take a gate. Cross the field ½ right, take the gate and continue ½ left to pass a coppice and a trig point on the right. Continue down the hill, to a narrow wood. Turn left along the footpath through the wood for 150m to join the B4089 'Captains Hill'.

3. Turn right and continue along the main road for 900m straight ahead, town centre joining Church Street to reach St Nicholas Church. Or to return to Spernal Lane, 30m after passing the shops and crossing Gunnings Road (continue at A).

A. *Take the footpath on the right, between the tennis court and the 'Greig', and continue into the park area. Follow the surfaced path alongside the river as it meanders and eventually reaches a tarmac path at a footbridge. Turn right and in 10m turn left and take a footpath to reach Arden Road. Cross the road and follow the path opposite, continuing alongside the river into open fields.*

B. *Follow the footpath alongside the river and around the field edge through 2 hedge gaps to a steel field gate. Take the gate and follow the river, then hedge on the left for 200m and take a gate on the left. Cross the field ½ right, take the gate to Church Farm drive and turn left. At the lane turn left for 300m and take the footbridge over river opposite Mill Ford House. Cross the field ½ right, take a gate and continue to take a gate into the lane opposite the coach entrance to Coughton Court.*

C. *Turn right along lane and follow the footpath to cross the river via a footbridge. Cross the lane and take the farm track opposite, marked the 'Arden Way', which curves right and climbs Windmill Hill and after 2.2km reaches Spernal Lane. Turn right and follow this sometimes busy lane for 400m until just past a farm track on the left, rejoin the Heart of England Way.*

Chapter 8

Section 22: Alcester to Bidford-on-Avon

Leaving Alcester to the south we are soon clear of the town and cross the River Arrow at the point where it is joined by the Alne. After crossing the A46, we reach farm buildings and turn left crossing the site of the Roman building. As we walk south, we have superb views across the Arrow Valley to Ragley Hall. This is the Marquess of Hertford's Palladian home, designed by Robert Hooke, built in 1680 and set in 'Capability' Brown parkland.

As we continue south we climb towards what the OS map designates Oversley Castle. Although it is believed that there was a Norman timber castle there, today the castle is a substantial private house, set in 65 acres of land, which was on sale in 2012 for £3.25m. Dropping down to Wixford we pass the church, dedicated to Saint Milburga of Wenlock, which was founded in the 12th Century.

We cross the car park to the Fish Inn and continue to Broom, crossing the main street next to the Broom Tavern. At both Wixford and Broom a right turn on the road next to either pub will take you to the return path, should you wish to shorten your walk.

Broom Tavern

Both Wixford and Broom had stations on the Birmingham – Gloucester Loop railway line. This line was opened in 1866 and closed in 1965 but connected Birmingham, Redditch, Alcester and Evesham, with stops at many small villages. Broom was quite a big station, as we will see on the return walk, as it provided the junction with the cross-country line to Stratford-upon-Avon. It is by the side of this line that we join the road to Bidford-on-Avon.

Bidford-on-Avon avoided being connected to the railway but the village has existed since at least roman times. Before the present bridge was built 600 years ago, the Romans established a ford close by. The source of the River Avon is at the village of Naseby in Northamptonshire from where it flows for 96 winding miles through Warwickshire, Worcestershire and Gloucestershire to the River Severn at Tewkesbury.

In the 20th century Bidford became popular with day trippers it is also claimed that William Shakespeare found their hospitality attractive. He is reputed, after a heavy nights drinking in a local hostelry, to have slept off the effects under a tree before making his way home. The ancient parish church of St Laurence, built in 1206, occupies a prominent position in the centre of the village overlooking the River Avon, as does the riverside pub The Frog.

Our return to Alcester, after a walk along the Salford Road, is along a bridleway. The bridleway is very pleasant on slightly higher ground, but on the approach to Broom crosses a cultivated field and may be heavy going when wet. On leaving the road from Broom, we follow the old railway line, passing the remains of the railway station platforms. After Wixford, the A46 conveniently provides the bridge over the River Arrow as we continue along the old railway, to return to Alcester.

Walk Directions

1. Commence opposite St Nicholas Church, from Church Street, take Malt Mill Lane and turn right into Gas House Lane. Opposite Chestnut Close turn left along the footpath across the park, to the Stratford Road. Cross the road and turn ½ left along the 'Old' road. Cross the River Arrow and turn right into Mill Lane and after 100m turn left into Primrose Lane and along the bridleway to cross the A46 footbridge and turn right.

2. Follow the concrete drive to Lower Oversley Farm and turn left at the farm along the track with the hedge on the left. Pass the invisible site

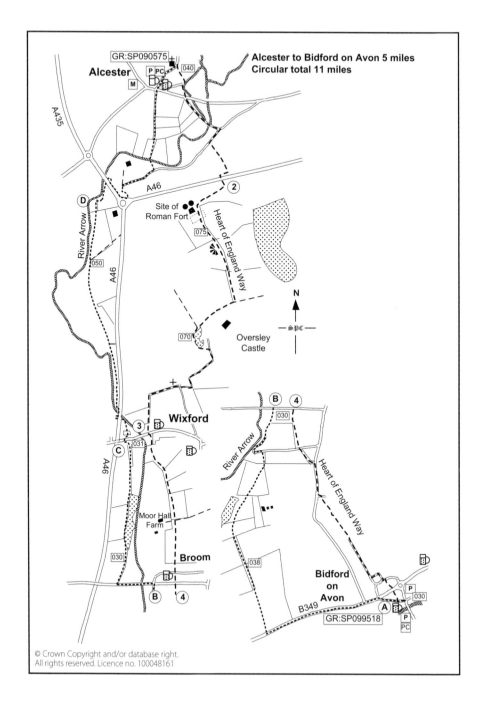

Alcester to Bidford on Avon 5 miles
Circular total 11 miles

of the Roman Fort and enjoy the view to Ragley Hall. Continue for 800m, climbing towards Oversley Castle and turn right, following the track around the hill to reach Oversley Castle entrance, and turn right. Continue down hill, along the track past Oversley Farm, over the 'cross roads' and past St Milburgas Church on the right. Continue along the track, then path behind the 'new' housing (ignore Church Fields path on left) and descend through the trees and turn left. Take a gate, then a 2nd gate through a caravan park, then a gate through the Fish Inn car park, at Wixford. Cross the road and take a stile (or, if preferred, turn right to follow instructions at 'C' to return to Alcester).

3. Follow the footpath alongside the river and take a bridge and stile. Continue along the top of the embankment, take a footbridge and then a stile and turn ½ right with the right fence. Continue with the fence, taking 4 stiles and crossing the track to Moor Hall Farm. Continue straight ahead and take a gate and follow the left hedge and then straight ahead to cross a field and take the stile right of the white house. Follow the footpath then drive, cross the road in Broom and continue along the lane opposite to cross the road, adjacent the Broom Tavern. Take the footpath right of 'The Ivy' (or, if preferred, turn right to follow instructions at 'B' to return to Alcester).

4. Follow the footpath to the recreation ground and keep to the right hedge. Pass right of the power pole to follow a footpath to take a gate. Cross the lane and take the footpath opposite to reach steps up to the road and turn right over the bridge of the old Stratford on Avon Midland Junction Railway. Take the next left, into Jackson's Meadow and immediately turn right and take the footpath. Continue along the footpath, which joins Westholme Road, then left into The Crescent. At the junction with Westholme Road, turn left and right to take the footpath which continues between properties over the B439 to reach High Street. At the High Street, turn left and right to reach the bridge over the River Avon or turn right to return to Alcester.

A. *Turn right along High Street to reach the B439 and turn left. Continue for 1km and, just past a layby, take the bridleway right, up the bank. Follow the track for 900m and take a gate. Cross the field ½ right, take a gate, and continue across the field ½ right. Enter a large field (crops) and cross ½ right, to a marker post and take the gate. Climb the bank, cross the bridge over the old Stratford on Avon Midland*

Junction Railway. Take a gate and follow the right fence, take the gate to the lane and turn left. Follow the lane around to the right, which becomes a bridleway to reach a road, adjacent an office block at Broom, and turn left along road.

B. *After 500m at a bridge-approach turn right along a concrete drive and take the stile right. Continue along right field edge, past the site of Broom Station, the junction of the Gloucester Loop Line (which ran from Barnt Green, south Birmingham to Gloucester) and the Stratford on Avon Midland Junction Railway. Although the old railway line through the woods has become a 'mountain bike trail', the right of way continues at the field edge, alongside the old railway line. Continue for 1300m, then take the gate and cross the road at Wixford.*

C. *Go around the 'armco' barrier, turn right down the bank, take a gate, turn left through an enclosure and take a stile. Follow the footpath alongside the river, under the A46 bridge. Take the steps up to the A46 and take the stile. Turn left alongside the carriageway, cross the river, take the stile and steps down the embankment and turn right along the path. Follow the path which becomes a track along the line of the old railway line. After 1200m take the new timber walkway and bridge, constructed in 2011, and continue along the top of the embankment. Follow the footpath to reach and take a gate at the river.*

D. *Turn right alongside the river to take a gate and continue under the A435 and turn right to take a gate and follow the footpath to the road. Turn left, follow the grass verge and continue around the roundabout to turn left into the bridleway. Take the gate, turn right along the lane for 300m and at the marker post take the footpath left over the river. Continue along surfaced footpath to join and continue straight ahead along the road, Bleachfield Street. Cross Stratford Road and turn right and left into Church Street and the starting point.*

Section 23: Bidford-on-Avon to Dorsington

Leaving Bidford we cross the ancient bridge and continue towards the village of Barton, passing the Cottage of Content pub. We now leave the road and climb along a good track, which gives views across the Avon Vale, and in the other direction our first view of Meon Hill. At

Barton Farm we follow field paths until reaching the lane to Dorsington. As we approach the village, walking along the narrow lane, looking to the right is Highfield House.

This is the impressive 15,000 square foot architect designed, green oak framed, 21st century home of Felix Dennis. The three level accommodation includes: normal domestic living; Caribbean/Treasure Island styled swimming pool, complete with palm trees and basement parking. Although the Way turns left at the village it is worth turning right for a few metres to see the superbly refurbished Old Manor House and adjoining house, also part of Felix Dennis's estate. As we continue through the village the buildings are a mixture of later construction as a serious fire, in 1754, destroyed the church and the buildings around it.

Our return to Bidford is back along the lane which passes Highfield Hall and then a footpath which may be heavy going when wet. The approach to the Bickmarsh Farm, which goes first through a wood and may be a little overgrown, crosses a cultivated field and is probably best accessed from the corner of the wood rather than along the diagonal right of way.

We walk along the Honebourne Road and then follow the quiet Bickmarsh 16 Acres Lane before dropping back down to walk through Marcliff. We now join the River Avon for a riverside walk, to return over the bridge to Bidford.

Walk Directions

1. From the junction of High Street and the B4085 Honeybourne Road cross the River Avon via the bridge and take the gate on the left, way marked Heart of England Way. Cross the field ½ right, to the right of the power pole, and take a gate. Continue straight ahead, take 2 gates and continue on a well marked path. Continue up the steps of the embankment between the river and the caravan site and turn right along a track, adjacent the weir, to reach the road and Barton.

2. Keep straight ahead along the road, past the Cottage of Content pub, and as road bends right take the track straight ahead. Follow the track curving left and climbing to give views left over the Avon valley and right to Meon Hill. Continue following the track turning right and left to reach Barton Farm.

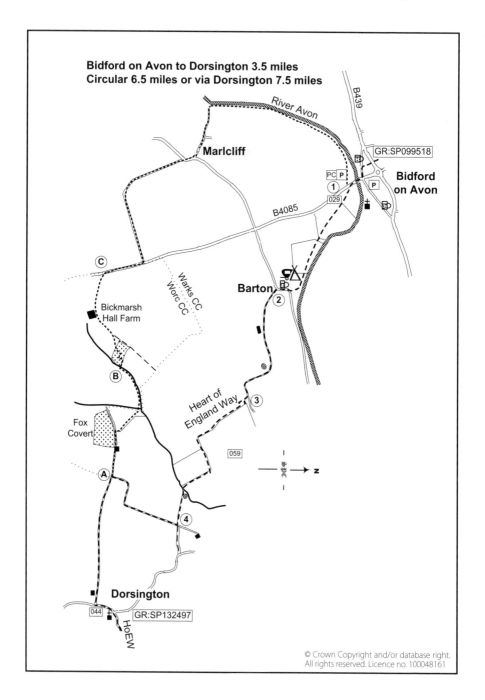

Bidford on Avon to Dorsington 3.5 miles
Circular 6.5 miles or via Dorsington 7.5 miles

River Avon

B439

Marlcliff

GR:SP099518

Bidford
on Avon

PC P

P

1

029

B4085

C

Warks CC
Worc CC

Barton

2

Bickmarsh
Hall Farm

B

Heart of
England Way

3

Fox
Covert

059

A

z

4

Dorsington

044

GR:SP132497

HoEW

3. At the farm leave the track and go right and left, past a way mark post, around the building perimeters, then turn right to follow the left hedge down hill. At the hedge corner, turn left and follow the left hedge. Continue through 2 hedge gaps and turn right to continue with the right hedge. Take the footbridge over the brook, turn left, take a gate, turn right and follow the right hedge, passing a pond. Continue up hill, take a stile and then gate to a bridleway.

4. Turn right along the bridleway and for 800m to reach a lane (alternatively if conditions are soft and bridleway is heavily horse trodden go straight ahead to the road and turn right to reach St Peters Church). At 'A' turn left to reach Dorsington, or turn right to return to Bidford-on-Avon. Follow the lane to reach Dorsington and turn left to reach the church to continue along the HoEW

A. *Leaving the HoEW follow the track, pass a cottage on the right and continue up the hill with Fox Covert on the left. Just over the brow of the hill take the stile on the right and continue with the right hedge. Cross left over the bottom corner of the field and take a footbridge. Continue with the brook on the right for 300m to reach and take a wide wooden bridge on the right.*

B. *Continue straight ahead from the bridge for 60m to take the footbridge on the left into the wood. Continue straight ahead to a track and turn right for 10m and then, following a way mark, turn ½ left. Follow the enclosure fence to the corner then straight ahead to exit the wood. Cross the field (crops) ½ right from the wood to turn left along a farm track to the corner of the Bickmarsh Farm complex. Continue around the perimeter of the farm to join a concrete drive leading to the road.*

C. *At the road turn right for 300m and turn left into Bickmarsh 16 Acres Lane. Follow this quiet lane as it bends right and then drops down to the village of Marlcliff joining the main road at a bend. Continue straight ahead and turn left into The Bank. Continue along the road to a fork and then straight ahead to take a track to reach the River Avon. Turn right, cross the footbridge, take a gate and continue alongside the River Avon to once again reach Honeybourne Road and turn left over the bridge to enter Bidford-on-Avon.*

Section 24: Dorsington to Long Marston

From the church in Dorsington, after a walk along a lane, we follow a footpath alongside Noleham Brook. The brook, which winds its way through the generally flat countryside, is at the north-eastern edges of the Vale of Evesham. The Vale has little industry, land use being mostly and traditionally agricultural and horticultural and including fruit farms, livestock farming and market gardening. The sheltered climate beneath the escarpment of the Cotswolds, the light alluvial soils and the ready availability of river water for irrigation also explain the high levels of vegetable production. There are also numerous orchards, survivors of a time when the entire Vale was covered with blossom in the spring.

At Long Marston we pass close to the Mason's Arms, crossing the road through the village to continue to Lower Quinton. The return route to Dorsington is quite a long circuit of 4.75 miles, almost entirely on footpaths through unpopulated countryside. However, about halfway we visit the Village of Pebworth, which apparently has a thriving Morris Dancing ensemble!

The focal point of the village is St Peter's church, which dominates the ridge on which Pebworth is set, and on a Sunday you may hear the full peal of its ten bells. The 13th century church has many items of interest – a Jacobean pulpit, a 15th century font, boxed pews and a particularly bitter epitaph to the scalded child of a previous vicar. It is a slight diversion from our route but the village has a pub, the Masons Arms. After leaving Pebworth we are soon back off road and can enjoy a couple more miles of countryside before reaching Dorsington.

Walk Directions

1. At St Peter's Church turn right along the lane, signed Braggington, for 250m, cross a bridge and take the stile right. Follow the field edge alongside the brook as the path continues between fences for 1200m and enters an open field. Continue with the right hedge, take the next gate and as the brook curves right follow a way marker and take a gate. Continue ½ left to a fence corner, continuing to a field corner, take a gate and cross the bridge. Continue with the left hedge, and at the end of a hedged corridor take a gate and turn left. Follow the left hedge, take 2 gates, follow the right fence (may be

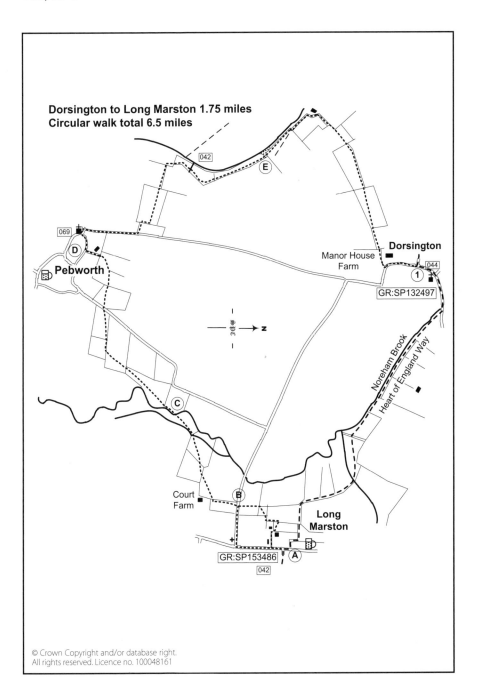

Dorsington to Long Marston 1.75 miles
Circular walk total 6.5 miles

042

E

069

D

Pebworth

Manor House
Farm

Dorsington

044

1

GR:SP132497

N

C

Noreham Brook

Heart of England Way

Court
Farm

B

Long
Marston

GR:SP153486

A

042

muddy!) take a gate and follow the path around the houses to Welford Road and turn right, close to the Mason's Arms.

A. *If ground conditions are good then after passing Wyre Lane take the right turn, at a finger post, to the end of the drive, turn right in front of the house and take a farm gate. Cross the field ½ left, take a stile, turn left with the fence to take a gate. Continue for a few metres, turn right to take a gate and left to a 2nd gate. Cross the field ½ right, take a gate and continue straight ahead to cross the field to the road. (Alternatively continue along road for 250m turn right along a lane, pass St James Church and in 200m take the stile on the left)*

B. *Cross the road, take the stile, bear right to follow the right fence and take the stile on the right. Cross the field ½ left, take a stile and bridge, continue ½ right and take the stile. Continue through a gap in the hedge line to a wooded corner of the field. Take the stile turn left to take the next stile, but if it is flooded at this point turn right for 60m, take a gate and return to the 2nd stile. Continue ½ left to take the bridge, turn left with the brook and take a gate.*

C. *Continue ½ right to the far end of this narrowing field, take a gate and bridge. Cross the field ¼ right, take a bridge and gate. Turn right, follow the hedge, take a gate and cross the field ½ left, take a gate to the road. Cross the road, take the gate, cross the field, take a gate and continue to take a gate left of the water trough. Continue to take the stile left of a bungalow, follow the footpath to the road and Pebworth.*

D. *Turn right along the road to St Peter's Church and then turn right along the lane to Dorsington. Continue to the bottom of the hill and at a finger post take the gate on the left. Follow the left hedge, take a gate and turn right to follow the right hedge then, at the halfway point turn left to cross the field. Take a gate, continue with the right hedge to take a further gate and turn right. Take the stile ahead, turn right, with the hedge and cross a concrete bridge. Continue left around the field's right perimeter, through a gate, to reach the far corner. Take a hurdle and then a hurdle in the corner at the end of the field.*

E. *Follow the left perimeter around the field to turn right in front of the corner gate. Continue right, for a short distance, to take a gate on the left along a track. Follow the fenced track to the next gate and take the pedestrian gate on the right. Follow the path between the hedge and the fence, (ignore the gates on the left) and take a gate. Turn right, in front of a farm gate, to take a pedestrian gate and continue around the field between the fences and take a stile. Cross the field, take a gate, follow the left hedge along a raised bank and take a gate. Cross the field from a way mark post ¼ right, to the field corner and take a gate. Follow the right hedge, take a gate, continue with the left hedge and take a gate to the road. Turn left to reach Dorsington and continue to the church.*

Section 25: Long Marston to Mickleton

As we leave Long Marston we soon cross a 'green way route' from Stratford-upon-Avon. This is old Great Western Railway line from Stratford-upon-Avon which, in its day, ran from Birmingham straight through to Cheltenham. However, less than ½ mile away, a length of this railway line still exists (the return route crosses it) connecting, so the OS Map tells us, the Central Engineering Park with the Worcester to Oxford line at Honeybourne. The Army sold the depot, which was one of its main strategic supply centres, many years ago but, behind the 3½ miles of perimeter fence, the 20 miles of rail track remains, full of rolling stock and locomotives.

This is the base of one of the countries railway stock leasing companies. For some of the stock, the obsolete and the no longer fashionable, it is its last resting place, whilst other still modern equipment is mothballed or being renovated. There is an annual open day and train spotter anoraks have populated the internet with their photographs of the old liveries and aging stock. If you Google Peter Tandy you will find, amongst his collection of railway photographs, a record of each train movement on and off the site.

Next we pass through Lower Quinton and then gradually climb, crossing the Green on the way, to Upper Quinton to rejoin our cross-country route. We are now on the lower slopes of Meon Hill, at the top of which is an Iron Age fort of impressive proportions, on which archaeologists have discovered finds from as early as the Stone Age through to the Roman periods. The hill has attracted tales of witchcraft and legend. Perhaps not a good idea to be too late on our walk lest we see the phantom hounds of the Celtic King Arawyn hunting the hill at night.

One true tale, which it has been suggested involved witch craft, was the murder, on St Valentines Day 1945, of Charles Walton, a 74 year-old farm labourer. He was found on the hill brutally murdered with his own trouncing hook embedded in his throat and his pitch fork pinning his body to the ground. The local police got nowhere with their investigations so Robert Fabian, of Scotland Yard, was brought in. This man inspired a post war television detective series, *Fabian of the Yard*, making him the first television police hero. Despite his notoriety the case was never solved. Perhaps it is as well that there is no public access to disturb the ghosts at the top of the hill.

If is a clear day, then a sweep of the horizon from south to north will reveal the summits of the Cotswold Ridge, Cleeve Hill, Prescott Hill, Bredon Hill and the Malverns. We arrive in Mickleton, which sits at the northern end of the steep scarp, and marks the western edge of the Cotswold Hills. Its place on the 'border' is characterised by the mix of buildings, some built of mellow Cotswold stone sitting next to the traditional black and white buildings of the Vale. The village has

St Lawrence Church Mickleton

two pubs, the Butchers Arms and Kings Arms, and also the Three Ways Hotel, the home of the famous Pudding Club, which preserves the tradition of 'the Great British Pudding'.

The Way takes us around the east side of the village and reveals the best view of the impressive church of St Lawrence. Its origins are 12th century, although records show that there was a church here in 960. The church is well worth a visit, particularly if you park next to it when you can also pay their voluntary parking fee.

Our return to Long Marston consists of two long cross-country sections. The first route is easily followed, although crops adjacent Abbots Ground Farm may give need for a slight detour from the straight route to reach the gap between the barns. The area around the single barn, further on, may present the opportunity to forge a path between the crop and the natural vegetation.

The second section commences with a road and rail crossing. The railway line links the Long Marston Marshalling Yards, mentioned earlier, with the Honeybourne junction on the Worcester – Oxford main line. If a train is seen approaching we can assured its pace will be pedestrian. After crossing the line we pass though Priory Farm, which has been undergoing re-development and touch on Broad Marston. We now head back across fields to Long Marston, crossing Noleham Brook, and retracing, in a reverse direction, the path to Pebworth.

Walk Directions

1. Continue south along Welford Road for a few metres and turn left into Wyre Lane. Keep straight along the lane to cross the 'Greenway' (the line of the old GWR Stratford – Gloucester line) and take the gate. Continue along the track, cross the bridge and continue with the right fence as the track turns left. Take the stile and follow the fenced footpath along the side of Long Marston Airfield. The path eventually turns right and terminates, take the stile on the left. Follow the right edge of the field and take a stile in the corner and turn left to take a gate into a field. Turn right and follow the right fence around the field to take stile and cross the road (B4632).

2. Go through a gap and follow the ditch and take 2 gates to reach a stile on the right. Take the stile and bridge and cross the field ½ left. Take a stile, bridge and gate and cross the field. Take a gate

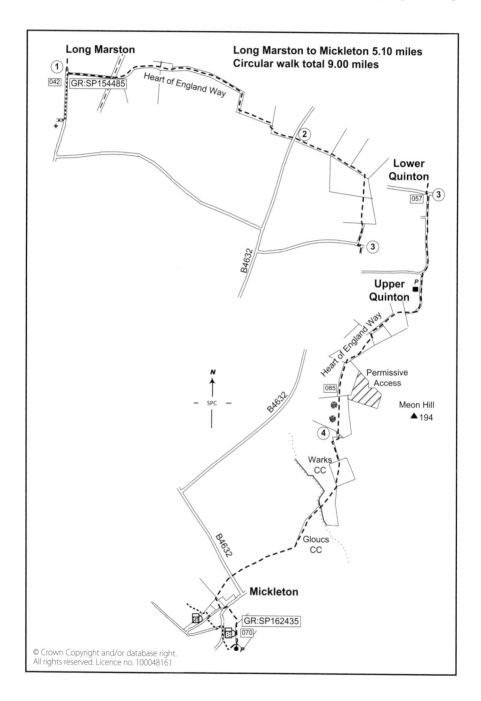

Long Marston

①
042 GR:SP154485

Heart of England Way

**Long Marston to Mickleton 5.10 miles
Circular walk total 9.00 miles**

②

**Lower
Quinton**

057 ③

③

B4632

**Upper
Quinton** P

Heart of England Way

085

Permissive
Access

N

SPC

B4632

Meon Hill
▲194

④

Warks
CC

B4632

Gloucs
CC

Mickleton

GR:SP162435
070

and bridge, follow the footpath and turn left over a bridge and then right along Aylstone Close to the junction with Main Road at Quinton. Turn left and right into Goose Lane

3. Continue along Goose Lane and left into Hill Lane and 'the Green' of Upper Quinton. At the end of the surfaced lane, take a gate on the right, follow the path and take a gate. Cross the field to a hedge corner and continue with the hedge on the right to take a gate. Continue straight ahead to the end of a fenced corridor and take the gate on the left. Climb the field to take a gate on the right and turn left and right around the field to take a gate on the left. Turn right and continue with the hedge on the right, take 2 gates and cross the field via a line of trees.

4. Take the gate and continue through a small wood, take a gate and turn right with the hedge on the right. Take a gate, turn left, and continue with the hedge on the left. Take the stile, cross the field ½ right and take the stile. Cross the field ½ left and take the gate. Continue with the fence on the right, take a stile, cross the field ½ left and join a track. Follow the track to the road (B4632). Cross the road, take the stile, cross the field and take the gate into Mickleton's recreation ground. Cross the space ½ left and take a gate to Back Lane. Turn left, and left into the B4632 at the butcher's shop. Cross the road and turn right into a narrow lane. At the end of the lane take a gate into a meadow, turn right and follow the right boundary to take the gate into the church yard of the church of St Lawrence.

A. *From the church turn right along the lane to High Street, turn right then left into Chapel Lane. At a finger post on the right, take the walled footpath between buildings and then turn right along Back Lane. At a finger post turn left along a wide walled footpath to reach an open field and turn left along a triangular grassed area to marker post.*

B. *Turn right to cross the field and take a bridge. Cross the field ½ left, to the corner and turn to follow the right hedge. Take a bridge, cross the field passing right of an old shed towards a line of trees. At the 2nd shed, continue with the ditch on the right, take a stile and cross the field, then track at Abbots Ground Farm (if crops obstruct go right and left to reach the barns) and continue between 2 barns.*

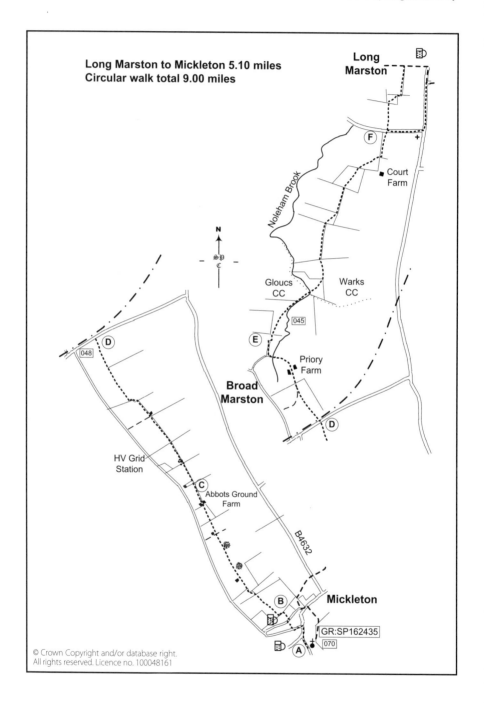

Long Marston to Mickleton 5.10 miles
Circular walk total 9.00 miles

Long Marston

Court Farm

F

Noleham Brook

N

Gloucs CC   Warks CC

045

D

048

E

Priory Farm

Broad Marston

D

HV Grid Station

C

Abbots Ground Farm

B4632

B

Mickleton

GR:SP162435

070

A

C. *Take the gate, follow the right hedge and take 2 stiles then a bridge to reach a barn. Go left around the barn to reach and follow the right hedge. Cross a bridge continue with right hedge, cross track to an adjacent barn and cross the bridge. Turn left along the field edge to reach a ditch and turn right and follow the ditch to the end of the hedge. Continue along the same line, pass a power pole and a single tree and take a stile to the road.*

D. *Cross the road and railway line (serves only Long Marston Storage Depot) via the stiles. Cross the field joining a track and take the gate adjacent a cattle grid. Continue along the track then surfaced lane through Priory Farm, cross a bridge and after 30m turn right along a track. Continue along the track to reach a hurdle, which may have a boggy approach. Take the hurdle and turn right into the field.*

E. *Turn left along the hedge to go through the gap in a 'hedge' line ahead. Now cross the field ½ right to join and follow the line of the brook. Take a hurdle and continue along the line of the brook to reach a gas-line marker post, at a bridge. Cross the bridge then cross the field to the corner, right of the next gas-line marker post. Take a stile, turn left to cross the field to take a stile at a hedge/fence junction. Continue with the right hedge and take a stile. Cross the field ½ right, take a stile and follow the right hedge to take a stile. Cross the field ¼ right and take a stile and bridge combination. Cross the field ½ right, take a stile and turn left to follow the left fence via stile to a road.*

F. *From this point, if undertaking the walk in 'winter conditions', the recommended route is to turn right along the road to reach Welford Road and turn left to reach the starting point. Alternatively cross the road, enter the field via the gate, cross straight ahead and take the gate. Turn ½ right, take a corner gate, then the next gate and in 5m turn left at a marker post and take the next gate. Follow the right hedge to meet the Heart of England Way and turn right to return to start.*

Chapter 9

Section 26: Mickleton to Mickleton Hills Farm

From Mickleton we make the biggest climb, since the start at Cannock Chase, as we tackle the Cotswold Hills. As we continue towards Mickleton Hills Farm, we may hear the sound of a distant train horn as it enters the 'secret tunnel' on the Worcester - Oxford railway, the site of the last battle between civilian armies. At the surface, the tree lined hump either side of Furze Lane follows the line of the 800m long tunnel 50m below us. We cross the north tunnel entrance as we turn away from the Mickleton Hill Farm, but the depth of vegetation may hide the line below.

Construction of the tunnel commenced in 1846 and it certainly proved a very tough engineering challenge for the civil engineers of the day. The Oxford, Worcester and Wolverhampton Railway, otherwise known as the old Worse and Worse, had appointed Brunel as their engineer. But after 3 years of unsatisfactory progress, in 1849, Brunel sacked the first contractor. It was another 2 years before the next contractor, Robert Marchant, an ex-Brunel assistant, was appointed and recommenced the project. However, by June of that year, disputes over the terms of contract, payment and ownership of the original contractor's plant lead to Brunel taking possession of the works and appointing a new contractor. Marchant, however, was having none of it. He declined to accept the termination of his contract and refused to hand over the works or plant, for which he maintained he had paid £10,000, and kept his men on site to guard 'his' property.

The new contractor, who was constructing the rest of the line, made several attempts to force the issue but at each attempt Marchant and his men drove them off. Brunel decided to take matters into his own hands and took charge. On Friday, July 20th he went to the tunnel with a large body of men he had gathered from his other railway projects in the region. Marchant had caught wind of Brunel's intentions and informed the local magistrates and urged them to take action. They attended and read the 'Riot Act' and Brunel was persuaded to retire. However Brunel was still determined to gain control of the tunnel and over the weekend more than 2000 men from his other midland contracts had continued to arrive, determined to evict the 150 Marchant men. When Brunel returned on the Monday morning, finding the magistrates had gone, a general attack took place and several heads were broken and other less serious injuries sustained. Marchant equally determined summoned the magistrates again, who returned with 36 policemen. The Riot Act was read again and Marchant, in the face of the continuing violence, approached Brunel and suggested they agree to refer the matter to arbitration which was accepted, just before the arrival of troops from Coventry

After the settlement of this, the last of England's civil disruptions, the Oxford, Worcester and Wolverhampton Railway Company asserted that the men under Brunel's direction had rioted in the causes of loyalty to their employers in trying to take possession of the works but without absolute violence or injury to individual persons - despite the menacing conduct of the contractor. Times were obviously different then; 'force majeure' in my contracting days was 'some unforeseen, unavoidable outside event as to make a contract unenforceable', rather than the violent conduct of the employer.

The tunnel was completed by the Spring of 1852 and, to bring matters up to date, the central section of the Cotswold line, as the railway is now known, is to be re-instated as a dual line 30 years after it was reduced to a single track. In July 2009 a 130-strong team of engineers worked around-the-clock in the tunnel, taking up the track and 20,000 tonnes of stone ballast. The existing stone was cleaned and re-laid with the addition of 50,000 tonnes of fresh stone to support 14,000 sleepers and the new twin tracks.

From Mickleton Hills Farm the Way continues right to Chipping Campden, but to return to Mickleton we turn left and continue downhill before beginning a long climb to the top of Stoke Hill, which is partly in Warwickshire and, thus, the highest summit in the county. On our way we go through the charming small village of Hidcote Boyce and then continue along a track, which winds up the hill giving stunning views on a clear day.

From the transmitter station we descend and cross the car park to the National Trust's Hidcote Gardens. The gardens were developed in the Arts and Crafts style as a series of outdoor 'rooms' by an American, Lawrence Johnston, whose family came to live in England. He started work on the gardens after being seriously wounded in the First World War and spent 40 years on the project.

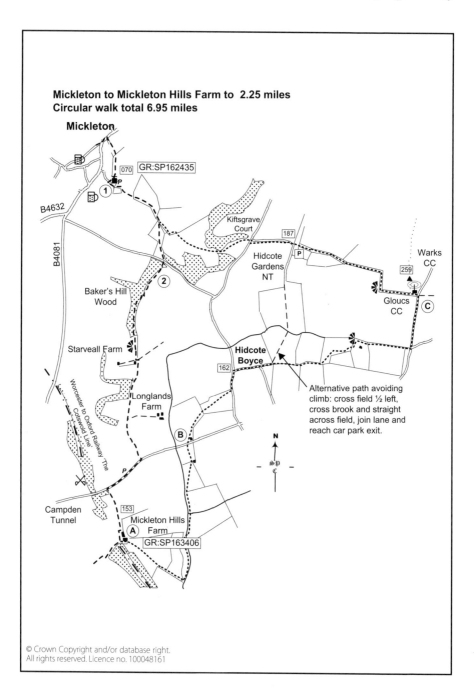

Mickleton to Mickleton Hills Farm to 2.25 miles
Circular walk total 6.95 miles

Mickleton

070   GR:SP162435

B4632

B4081

Kiftsgrave Court

187

Hidcote Gardens NT

P

Warks CC

259

Gloucs CC

C

Baker's Hill Wood

2

Starveall Farm

Hidcote Boyce

162

Alternative path avoiding climb: cross field ½ left, cross brook and straight across field, join lane and reach car park exit.

Worcester to Oxford Railway The Cotswold Line

Longlands Farm

B

N

Campden Tunnel

153

Mickleton Hills Farm

A

GR:SP163406

On our way down to Mickleton we pass Kiftsgate Court, built at the end of the 19th century. Its distinctive gardens were started in the 1920s by Heather Muir and development has continued by the successive two generations of Muir women.

Walk Directions

1. From the church go to the entrance to the lane and turn left up the stone track and take the pedestrian gate. Follow the wall on the right and from the corner turn ½ right to pass the large tree on the left and take the gate ahead. Follow the right hedge around the field and take the gate and continue 20m to take the stile/bridge on the right. At the top of the bank go ½ left to pass the fence corner, continue to the top corner of the field take the gate and cross the road.

2. Climb the steps up the bank, take a gate, turn right and follow the right field edge then into the wood as the climb levels out. Follow the path as it winds through the woods at the top of the scarp edge. As the path exits the wood follow the left hedge to a track and a barn, turn left and right along a 'surfaced' track. Continue to a lane, turn right along lane for 350m. Take the drive on the left to Mickleton Hills Farm. Turn right and left at the farm house to cross the wide grass area and reach the fence over the entrance to Campden Hill Railway Tunnel, turn right to continue along the HoEW or left to return to Mickleton.

A. *Take 2 gates, cross the field ½ right, pass the concrete marker posts to the fence corner and continue with the right fence. Take a gate and continue to turn left in front of the next gate. Follow the path, cross the brook and continue around the field edge with a further brook and the hedge on the right. Almost at the end of the narrow field, cross a bridge on the right and turn left. Continue at the left field edge following the line of the brook, crossing a bridge then a plank bridge. Cross the field (crops) ½ right to reach the barn. Take the gate on the left and follow the track to take a gate and cross the road.*

B. *Continue along the left side of a barn, then follow the right hedge to the hedge gap at the field corner and turn left to take the stile on the right. Cross the field ½ left to the corner and take the stile to the road. Turn left along the road and then turn right through Hidcote Boyce.*

Continue straight ahead, pass a spring fed trough and take the gate.
Follow the right fence (see the map for an alternative route directly to
Hidcote Gardens avoiding the climb) and take the gate to join the
track. Take 2 further gates, enter a field and follow the vehicle track
winding up the field to take a gate. Turn left and climb the bank to
pass a marker post and continue right with the left hedge to take a
gate. Follow the wide path, take a gate and stile to the road. Turn left
to reach the Communications Building and turn left along the track.

C. *Take a gate and continue right and left, then down hill along the*
track to the Hidcote Garden car park. Cross the car park and
continue along the road. After a few metres take the hedge gap left
and follow the footpath parallel to the road. Take a gate, cross the
field ¼ left and take the gate to the road. Turn right for 30m and
take the blue gate on the left. Continue down the centre of the field,
then through a narrow gap between the woods. Now follow the
contour and on line of church steeple drop down to take a gate. Turn
left around field edge to return via 2 gates to the church.

Section 27: Mickleton Hills Farm to Broad Campden

After leaving Mickleton Hills Farm, continuing along the Way, we soon
reach the old wool merchants town of Chipping Campden. We first
pass the land mark church of St James, which was established by the
Normans. However, rebuilt in the 15th century in the perpendicular
style, it is regarded as the most beautiful example of a wool church.
Next door is the impressive Gateway to the 17th century Campden
House which was burnt down during the civil war.

Arriving in the centre of the town, I would not argue with their
opinion that they have the most beautiful High Street in England.
Although Chipping Campden can trace its history back to Saxon times
it was in the 14th century that the locally produced wool, from the
Cotswold sheep, established the town as the areas wool trading centre.
The wealth that this generated, is there to be seen in all of the
splendid buildings that exist today.

After Chipping Campden we soon reach the small and quiet
backwater village of Broad Campden and pass its Quaker Meeting
House, small Victorian church and the highly recommended pub, the
Baker's Arms. Our return to Mickleton Hills Farm takes us first to
Paxford, another small village.

Chipping Campden

However, just before we reach the village, a new wood has sprung up and the new rides have diverted the right of way shown on the OS map. In the village we pass the Churchill Arms and, as we leave, we pass a Point to Point horse racing course which, according to my research, is an Easter event.

Continuing across the fields to Ebrington where we pass Ebrington Arms, which was the CAMRA, North Cotswold Pub of the year in 2009 and 2010. The narrow lane through the village, leads us to a path to the impressive church of St Eadburgha. From Ebrington we follow a quiet lane which turns into a road approaching the railway line. Just before we turn from the road, to complete the cross-country return to our start, we pass Battledene Farm and, I assume, its name recognises the Brunel hostilities.

Walk Directions

1. From the head of the tunnel follow the left fence line down hill, to take a gate. Turn right with the hedge to the corner, turn left and follow the hedge for 800m, turning left at the field corner. Continue in the field, with the right hedge, to take a gate on the right and follow the fenced path around the school perimeter to join a drive

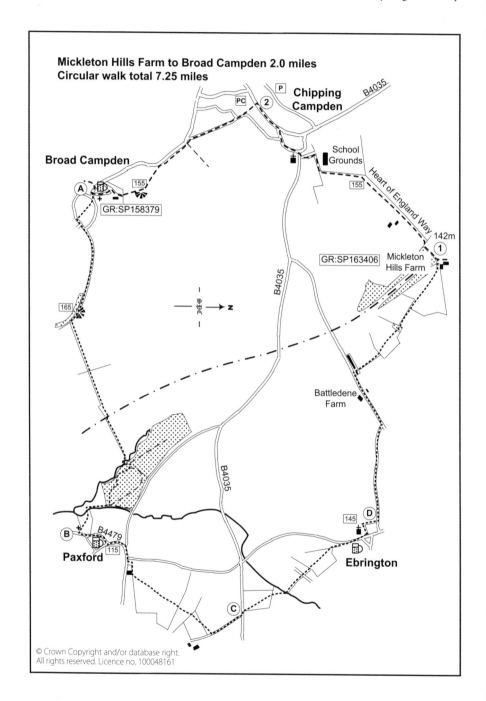

Mickleton Hills Farm to Broad Campden 2.0 miles
Circular walk total 7.25 miles

Chipping Campden

B4035

P

PC

2

School Grounds

Broad Campden

Heart of England Way

A

155

155

GR:SP158379

142m

1

165

GR:SP163406

Mickleton Hills Farm

B4035

Battledene Farm

B4035

145

D

B

B4479

115

Ebrington

Paxford

C

and turn left to the road. Turn right and follow road into the centre of Chipping Campden.

2. In Lower High Street turn left through the Noel Arms Hotel old coach entrance. Walk straight ahead through the yard and turn right along George Lane. Follow the lane, as it narrows, for 500m and at the road junction turn left and right across a farm drive and follow the right hedge. At the right bend in the hedge go ½ left over the summit of the field and, curving right, reach and take the gate. Follow the path for a few metres along the right fence and cross the drive left to take a gate opposite. Continue along the walled path, then the lane to pass St Michael and All Angels Church to the road junction in Broad Campden. Turn right to continue the HoEW.

A. *At the junction turn left and right to take the path beyond the 'unsuitable for motors' sign to a lane. Turn left and follow the lane, signed Paxford, to the summit of the hill. Continue for a further 200m and take the stile on the left. Follow the right hedge, take a gate and after 800m cross the railway. Continue with the hedge and, before the end of the field, take the gate on the right. Turn left and continue to the field corner, turn right for 30m, take the bridge on the left to a 'new' wood. Turn left towards the hedge gap and right to follow the wide ride to the right and reach a footpath at a brook. Turn right, take a stile, follow the brook and cross the bridge. Cross the field ½ right, take a stile and turn left along the road into Paxford.*

B. *Pass the Churchill Arms and follow the main B4479 road out of Paxford. Pass a lane on the left, signed Ebrington, and take the left hedge gap. Follow the left hedge around a 'garden' to take the hedge gap left to the field. Continue with the right hedge to a power pole. From the pole cross the field ½ right (crops), on a line 50m left of a 'windmill' and continue to take the gap in the hedge opposite. On the same line cross straight down the field, take a gate, cross the next field ½ left to take a gate. Continue to a drive at a marker post, turn left along drive and take the stile to the road.*

C. *Turn left for 20m, take a gate right and cross the field ½ left to take a bridge right of the field corner. Continue straight ahead to take a bridge over a brook. Follow the right hedge, take the stiles then a bridge. Cross the field to the corner, take the stiles and turn right with the hedge to the lane. Turn right to Ebrington, pass the Ebrington Arms, join the left footpath and take the signed path to St Eadburghas Church. From the church take the right footpath to Campden Road and turn left.*

D. *Follow the lane to the T-junction and turn left. After 450m turn right along a bridle way. Take the gate follow the right hedge, through a gap. Cross the field ½ left, continue through a plantation and take a gate to the field. Follow the left hedge, take a gate and cross the field, via the concrete marker posts, turning left through 2 gates at the farm buildings and return to the HoEW.*

Section 28: Broad Campden to Blockley

From opposite the Baker's Arms the Way takes us on a climb up the hills of the old Northwick Park Estate. At the summit we cross Five Mile Drive, which runs from the Grade 1 Listed Northwick Hall. Inexplicably, according to the OS map, the drive turns left and becomes the A44! Today the hall is an apartment complex and the adjacent area a business park.

We now continue gently downhill before steeply descending, crossing and climbing out of one of the many streams that cut through the Cotswold Hills, to arrive in Blockley. This village is said to be one of the Cotswold's best kept secrets and yet another gem along the Way. If we take a slight detour from the Way and turn left by the Church, we can visit the village shop. This is owned

St Peter and St Paul Church Blockley

by the community who opened it in 2008 when it was realised that the last shop in the village was closing. It has a post office, newsagent and sells local produce, with its own bakery and café.

Blockley early history is fairly similar to other Cotswold villages but after the decline of the wool trade it became a prosperous centre for the production of silk. The silk boom was short lived but it is the architecture of the period which enables it to stand apart from any of the other Cotswold villages.

The church of St Peter and St Paul is another impressive buildin,g founded in 1170, and inside it has memorials to the Northwood Park families, two by the eminent 18th century sculptor John Michael Rysbrack. The Great Western Arms pub, a traditional pub owned by Hook Norton Breweries, is a reminder of the village's pretence at once being on a railway line, even though its railway station was 1.5 miles away.

Our return to Broad Campden reveals the unique nature of Blockley's architecture, as we walk along its mile-long narrow main street with raised pavements, small cottages, old mill buildings and the Crown, a 14th century coaching inn. At the end of the street we follow a bridleway and climb through woods and then enjoy the view of the impressive Upton Wold Farm House. We continue over Northwick Hill and cross the slightly overgrown Five Mile Drive. As we join the track from the Stanleys Quarry entrance road, a view to the left through the hedge will reveal Chipping Campden below us and Meon Hill beyond.

Walk Directions

1. Opposite the Baker's Arms take the track alongside the high wall on the left and take the gate. From the corner, continue with the wall then a hedge to the end of the hedge and on the same line cross the field to take a stile. Cross the corner of the field ¼ right, through a hedge gap. Continue on the same line up the hill to pass between an enclosure on the left and a stone wall on the right. Follow the wall/fence and take a gate. Pass a gate on the right, turn left along the side of the buildings at Campden Hill Farm. Follow the path, take a gate, reach a track and turn left. Follow the track up the hill to reach and cross Five Mile Drive ½ left to continue along the track.

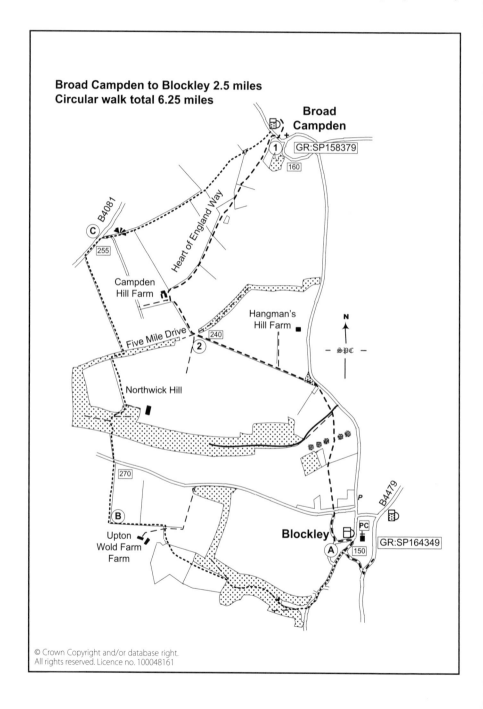

Broad Campden to Blockley 2.5 miles
Circular walk total 6.25 miles

Broad Campden — GR:SP158379

160

B4081

Heart of England Way

C — 255

Campden Hill Farm

Hangman's Hill Farm

N

Five Mile Drive — 240 — 2

Northwick Hill

270

B — Upton Wold Farm Farm

B4479

P

Blockley — PC — A — 150 — GR:SP164349

2. Follow the track, with a stone wall on the right, for 900m where the track becomes a path entering a wood. Follow the path right and left and take 2 gates into a field. Go down hill, take a stile and cross a stream via bridge. Follow the track right then immediate ½ left, climb the hill through a line of trees, to the top. Go along the side of an enclosure fence on the right. Take a stile, continue straight on through a hedge gap and then a hedge gap into a field. Cross the field ¼ right, take a stile and follow the path to Greenway Road. Cross the road to follow Back Ends, then 1st left down Bell Bank and right into High Street, opposite the lane to St Peter and St Paul Church. Turn right either to continue the HoEW or return to Broad Campden.

A. *Continue along High Street for 600m and adjacent the Royal Mail post box take a 'Private Drive' signed Warren House on the right. Continue up the hill, pass a house, as the drive becomes track. Ignore a left turn (the Diamond Way), continue up the hill for 500m and where the track continues to the right steeply up hill, take a gate on the left at the corner of the wood. Turn right follow the edge of the wood and take a gate. Continue straight ahead to marker post and turn ½ right up hill take a gate. Turn left to follow the wall up hill around the field. Cross the drive to Upton Wold Farm, then through a gap in the wall and turn left. Follow the wall on the left and turn right at the 2nd wall gap.*

B. *Follow wall on the right for 450m and cross the lane at the gates. Follow the track opposite down hill, as it bends left and right through the woods, then up hill into field. Continue with the left wall, then into the woods at Five Mile Drive. Turn right at a marker post, continue along the path for 100m and turn left at a marker post. Leave the wood and follow the left stone wall to reach the B4081. Turn right and follow the road for 200m to turn right into Stanley Quarry entrance.*

C. *Continue straight ahead and, where the quarry road turns right, take a gate onto a farm track. Enjoy the views north to the truncated top of Meon Hill and beyond to Avon Vale. Follow the track down hill to the end of the hedge on the left. Continue straight ahead as the track crosses the field and take a gate at a wood. Continue along the track to reach the road at Broad Campden and turn right for the Bakers Arms.*

Chapter 10

Section 29: Blockley to Batsford

As we continue along the Way, down School Lane past Blockley's only commercial attraction, the Mill Gardens, we cross Blockley Brook. After leaving the road the path climbs steeply to reach our last summit on the Way. The view back to Blockley is well worth the pause to enjoy and gain your breath. Crossing the lane is also another milestone, as this is the watershed between the rivers Avon and Thames. All the rainfall and various springs along the Way now find a route to the Rivers Dickler, or Eye, which join the Windrush at Bourton-on-the-Water which continues to the Thames.

As we descend the hill we come to Batsford Arboretum and Garden Centre. Although Batsford Park's history can be traced back to the17th century, it was in the 19th century that Algernon Bertram Freeman, later Lord Redesdale, or Bertie as he was known, started the rebuilding and landscaping that can be seen today.

Bertie was an attaché to the foreign office and travelled widely in Asia, where he became fascinated by the landscapes of China and Japan. Between 1888 and the early years of the 20th century he demolished the Georgian house, rebuilt a new mansion and re-landscaped the park. He established 'wild gardens' of natural planting in the Japanese style, together with rockeries, a stream, waterfalls and a unique bamboo collection. In 1984 the family donated the park to a charitable trust, which is continuing to develop the arboretum as a place of beauty for everyone to enjoy.

The return to Blockley takes us along a path at the edge of the park surrounding the House before we take a detour through the village of Batsford. The church of St Mary was built in 1861, predating Bertie's influence, in the neo-Norman style. Standing in the village street it is easy to imagine that you had walked back to an earlier time as you anticipate the arrival of the Lord and Lady's carriage.

We climb back over the hill and enjoy more views as we descend through the Northwood Estate and continue through the village of Draycott, crossing the Blockley Brook to return to Blockley.

Walk Directions

1. From High Street, with the Church on the left, proceed along the road and turn left into School Lane. Continue to the B4479 and cross the road to turn left along a footpath at the side of the road. After 50m turn right along a track signed 'Heart of England Way' and take a stile into the field. Follow the left hedge/stream up hill, take a stile and continue ½ right and take a stile to Park Farm. Continue up hill ¼ left, keeping close to the left hedge, take a stile and turn left along the bridle way.

2. Take a gate and turn right into a field and follow the right hedge to cross the road (the line of the Severn/Thames watershed) and take the stile opposite. Follow the track for 900m, close to the left wall, through the woods. Continue down hill to reach a marker post, close to a house, and take a stile. Cross the field, take a gate, cross the drive ½ right and take a gate. Bear left across to a wall and follow the wall to the corner, turn right to continue along the HoEW.

A. *At the corner of the wall turn left, through a gate and follow the left wall/field edge. Cross 3 fields and take a stile. Continue along the same line to take the stile on the left and behind a gate. Follow left field edge and continue along the fenced path to take a gate to the lane. Turn left along the lane and 1st left to the centre of the village of Batsford. At the next junction turn right and then 1st left, to climb the hill, and at the sharp left bend take the gate on the right.*

B. *Cross the field ½ left to take a corner gate, follow the right field edge and take the gate on the right signed 'Northwick Estates'. Follow the path through a plantation and continue straight ahead to take a stile. Follow the left fence, take a gate and continue with the fence to reach the corner of a wood projecting into the field. Continue at the edge of the field down hill to take a stile. Cross the field ½ right, cross a bridge, turn left and follow the marked footpath to a drive. Turn right along the drive to the road and turn left to Draycott.*

C. *At the cross roads continue straight ahead for 200m and at Kettles Barn turn left along the road then track, to reach a field. Cross the field ½ right, between the power poles, and take a gate in the corner to the road. Turn left along the road and after 80m take the stile on*

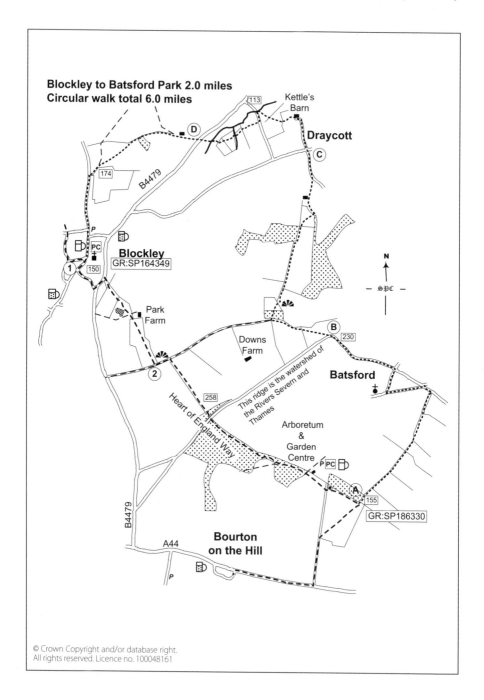

Blockley to Batsford Park 2.0 miles
Circular walk total 6.0 miles

Kettle's Barn

Draycott

113

174

B4479

P
PC

Blockley
GR:SP164349

150

Park Farm

Downs Farm

B
230

This ridge is the watershed of the Rivers Severn and Thames

Batsford

2

258

Heart of England Way

Arboretum & Garden Centre

P PC

A
155
GR:SP186330

B4479

A44

Bourton on the Hill

P

N

the right. Cross the field to take a stile left of the field corner. Cross the field ½ left, to cross a bridge. Now cross the field ½ right and take a stile and continue ½ right to take a stile to the drive. Follow the drive to the road.

D. *Cross the road, follow the drive opposite, pass a cottage and at the right bend take the stile on the left. Turn right, follow the right fence, cross a bridge, and continue through a wood and over a stile. Follow the wall on the right to the bend and now cross the field slightly left, to join a track from the right. Follow the track left and take the stile to the road. Turn left along the road to the centre of Blockley.*

Section 30: Batsford to Longborough

We turn acutely right to follow the Way, joining the main drive and turning right along the A44 to Bourton-on-the-Hill. The village, despite its small size, has a long history and two manor houses. Its church, anciently called St Mary's but now St Lawrence, was built in 1157. The parish registers go back to 1568 and are virtually complete. The name of the village pub, the Horse and Groom, a CAMRA entry, records the fact that from the 18th century to just before the Second World War Bourton Downs were noted for their horse racing stables.

Sezincote Park

The path from the village crosses a couple of fields before entering the old Sezincote Park. A glimpse of the house can be seen between the trees as we cross the drive to the house. After crossing the stream, and passing through the gate, although our natural view may be left to the ornamental lake, it is the view right up the hill, which reveals the house crouching above us. Its name is recorded in the Domesday Book and is derived from the Norman French *la chene* – the home of the oaks – and *cot* Old English for shelter. Thus the original Cheisnecote has derived as Sezincote.

The present house was built in 1810 for Charles Cockerell who inherited it from his older brother, both of whom had served in India with the East India Company. Keeping things in the family, it was another brother, Samuel Charles, a noted Architect and also a Surveyor to the East India Company, who designed the house. The house is unique, built in the Mogul Style of Rajasthan and was the inspiration for the Brighton Pavilion.

We continue along the footpath, which provides wide views across the wide Vale of Bourton to Longborough. The hills above the village were first settled over 5000 years ago, as evidenced by the Long Barrow. From Norman times the main manor of Longborough passed between powerful families, allied to royalty, and the church. In 1539 the manor was granted to Thomas Leigh, a former Lord Mayor of London and remained in the family until 1921.

The church of St James was built in the 12th century, elements of which survive. Like all of the churches along the Way it has been extended many times over the centuries. But it is worth a visit to see its two transepts. The south transept, built in the 14th century, contains effigies of the Leigh Family and the north Transept was built in 1822, as a private chapel for the Sezincote House and village, by S C Cockerell.

To return to Batsford we turn left at the Donnington Breweries pub, the Coach and Horses. The route takes us through the village to join a footpath that wanders through the Vale to Moreton-in-Marsh. The town has been a traveller's town for at least 1700 years as it both straddles the Fosse Way and, since 1853, has had a station on the Oxford to Worcester railway line. Moreton has also had a market since the 13th century and its wide main street, narrow burgage plots and back lanes are typical of many old towns. There is also no shortage of accommodation and hostelries to revive the weary traveller amongst the elegant 18th century inns and houses.

Many UK fire fighters will also be familiar with Moreton's charms as, since 1966, the old RAF base, just east of the town, has been the home of the Fire Service College which is known as the world's leading fire training college. The path west, to Batsford, takes us through the narrow lanes to follow a cross field footpath to complete our walk.

Walk Directions

1. From the end of the wall, cross the field ¾ right to meet the Batsford driveway. Turn left to the junction with the A44. Turn right, to Bourton on the Hill, and take the 2nd lane on the left at Corner Cottage. Continue along the lane and turn 1st right and then after 60m left along the footpath signposted 'Heart of England Way'. At a gate follow the right wall and take a gate. Cross the field, take a gate, then a stile and follow the right fence to take a stile.

2. From this point a barbed wired fence has been erected along the public footpath to separate people from the estate's 'friendly' cattle. At each old field boundary a field gate deflects us either to the left or right side of the fence. After crossing the surfaced drive, at the approach to the wood take the pedestrian gate to the narrow corridor next to the wood. Take the next gate, cross the stream, take a gate and continue to follow the fence line, passing below Sezincote House, climbing the hill and exiting the estate via the gate in the gap between the woods. Continue to cross the drive, follow the right hedge and take a gate. Cross a wood then follow the left fence through the fields, take 2 gates and follow a footpath then drive to the road at Longborough. Turn left and continue to the village green at the Coach and Horses (to return to Batsford go to A).

3. Turn right along High Street and continue for 300m and turn left into Banks Fee Lane. Follow the lane then track to a finger post and turn right to follow Heart of England Way footpath.

A. *Turn left, opposite the Coach and Horses, continue for 400m and turn left into Bean Hill signed 'Moreton in Marsh'. Follow the footpath between the houses and take a stile. Cross the field ½ right, take a stile, turn left, take stile and follow the left hedge to cross a bridge. Cross the field ¾ left, to a hedge gap and take the stile,*

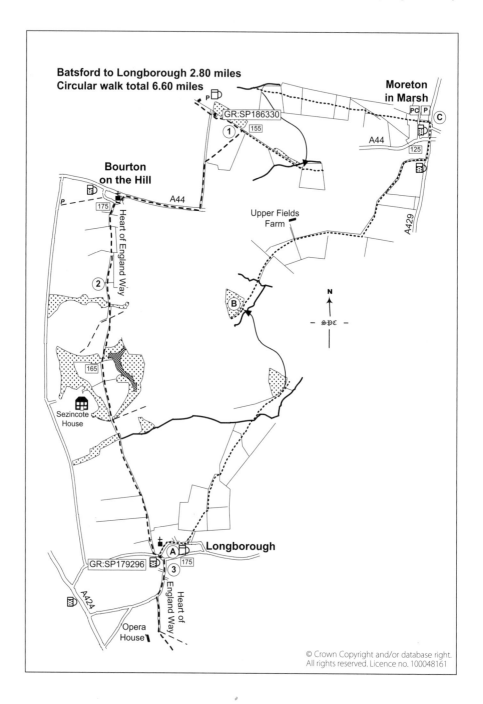

Batsford to Longborough 2.80 miles
Circular walk total 6.60 miles

GR:SP186330

Moreton
in Marsh

155

A44

125

Bourton
on the Hill

175

A44

Heart of England Way

Upper Fields
Farm

A429

2

B

165

N

— S♇C —

Sezincote
House

Longborough

A

GR:SP179296

3   175

Heart of
England Way

A424

Opera
House

continue on the same line, cross the field, take a stile and cross the bridge. Turn ½ right follow the line of the brook to a bend and continue across the field diagonally to meet the hedge. Turn right, follow the hedge then edge of the wood and take a gate.

B. *Cross the field, pass a way marked tree stump and take the gate. Follow the right hedge and take a gate. Follow the right hedge to the corner and cross the field ½ right to the far left corner and take a gate. Follow the left hedge through 2 fields and turn left through a gap in the hedge at a marker post. Follow the left hedge, take a gate and then a gate to a track. Follow the track, joining and continuing along Parkers Lane to the High Street and turn left to the centre of Moreton in Marsh.*

C. *After 300m turn left along Corders Lane, cross over the intersection with Hospital Road, take the footpath between the houses and take a gate. Cross the field ¼ left, to follow the left fence and take a gate on the left. Turn right, cross a bridge and take a gate. Follow the path across 5 fields, taking gates to reach a field corner. Take a gate, bear right, cross a bridge and follow the right hedge through 2 fields, taking 2 gates. Continue ahead for 50m to rejoin the end of the wall.*

Section 31: Longborough to Hyde Mill

We continue through Longborough, passing the village shop that also provides hot drinks and snacks. Turning from the High Street into Banks Fee Lane, we pass Longborough's second and smaller manor of Banks Fee, which has also been part of the village history since the Normans. The present house, built in 1753, surrounded by pleasure grounds and gardens, provides the venue for Longborough's annual six week season of Opera.

Turning from the bridleway we take a footpath across the fields, then through woods to climb to the site of the Battle of Stow. The accompanying map shows the position of the interpretation stone of this, the last battle of the civil war. It was the early morning of 21st March 1646 when, after the initial success of the royalists holding the high ground, the superior parliamentary forces attacked again, overwhelmed and routed the royalists. A running fight continued back to Stow, where the streets were said to have run with blood, and the

Donnington Brewery

royalist commanding officer, Sir Jacob Astley, was captured and conceded defeat.

We now continue along a series of quiet lanes and pass the 13th century watermill home of Donnington Breweries, where Thomas Arkell started brewing there in 1865. The brewery is still in the same family but unfortunately, there is no off licence or visitor centre. However, if you have not already tasted their beer at Moreton-in-Marsh or Longborough, the next chance is at Lower Swell. After crossing the River Dickler, we climb to Upper Swell and take care walking along the busy road and then cross the fields and parkland of the Abbotswood estate.

If you choose to take the short cut to Stow-on-the-Wold you will pass the entrance to the estate. But unfortunately neither reveals the 19th century, Sir Edwin Lutyens designed house and garden, although continuing along the Way, when we pass Lower Swell's village green, we can admire the Lutyens designed war memorial. However, before leaving the estate we pass close to the sacred spring of 'Ladys Well', which, according to legend, is visited at midnight to drink by the 'Horestone', an ancient boulder that rests in a field ¾ mile away.

If you choose not to take the B4068 either to visit the Golden Ball Inn or take another potential short cut to Stow-on-the-Wold, we follow a lane then track to Hyde Mill. On the Way we pass an enormous milking shed and barn before going gently downhill, with views across to Nether Swell Manor, and then cross a meadow to the Mill, which was mentioned in the Domesday Book.

Our return to Longborough skirts first around a large equestrian centre before passing through some of the cottages of Nether Swell Manor. The manor was built in 1903 and designed by Sir Guy Dawber, who was well known for his Arts and Crafts Designs, but it is now a series of separate private residences. After crossing the Fosse Way and climbing the hill we reach Stow-on-the-Wold.

Stow has been a settlement since at least 700BC at the junction of the ancient Jurasic Cotswold Ridgeway and the Salt Way. Before the Normans Evesham Abbey controlled the area and the Abbotts established Stow as a trading centre. Given Stow's high and exposed position, the construction of its large enclosed town square was probably encouraged to afford protection from the elements. There are a number of pubs, restaurants and cafes in the town, including Donnington Breweries' the Queens Head.

We leave the town along a lane which passes two of Stow's wells. It was not until 1937 that mains water was provided and until then all of the water was obtained from the wells. People either fetched water themselves or water carts distributed it to the townspeople for a farthing a bucket. Even today many people still prefer their drinking water from the well, as you may see when you pass.

The lane becomes a bridleway that joins a lane into the village of Broadwell, which has a large village green and the Fox Inn, another Donnington pub, sits at the side of it. We then leave the road and take a footpath that leads through the church yard of the impressive, 12th century church of St Paul with its unusual bale top tombs. We leave the village along a lane crossing the Fosse Way and continue to Donnington.

We can make a detour here to cross the village to see the Battle of Stow interpretation stone, where the parliamentarians succeeded in winning the day and the war. Continuing along the return path we enter a field and walk the perimeter of Donnington Manor's 'Ha Ha' wall. After another couple of fields we follow a bridleway which leads gently back to Longborough.

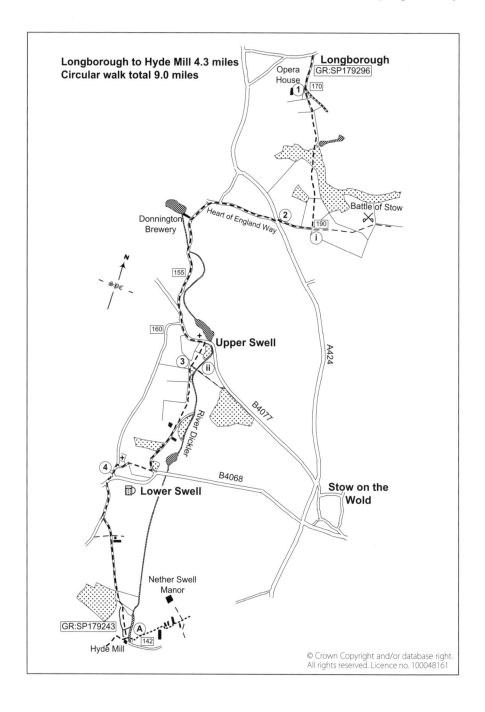

Longborough to Hyde Mill 4.3 miles
Circular walk total 9.0 miles

Opera House

Longborough
GR:SP179296
170

Battle of Stow

Donnington Brewery

Heart of England Way

2
190
i

N

spc

155

160

Upper Swell

A424

3
ii

B4077

River Dicker

4

B4068

Lower Swell

Stow on the Wold

Nether Swell Manor

GR:SP179243
A
142
Hyde Mill

Walk Directions

1. From the finger post, follow the footpath, take a stile, follow the right fence and take a stile, Cross the field close to the left fence take a stile then a bridge on the right and turn left. Follow the path climbing through a wood to reach an open meadow. Follow the left boundary of the open meadow and cross a bridge. Cross the field to take a stile and turn right and follow the track to the road. (See note (i) below for up hill route to Battle of Stow interpretation stone).

2. Cross the A424 and follow the lane signed 'Condicote' and take the 1st left signed 'Upper Swell'. Follow the lane, passing the Donnington Brewery and crossing the River Dickler. At the junction with the B4077, turn left and continue through the village of Upper Swell taking care along this busy narrow road. Continue down hill and just before the right hand bend take the signed footpath right. Take a gate, cross the field, take a gate and continue and cross the field to the corner of the wood and take a gate. (See note (ii) below for the short cut to Stow-on-the-Wold via the Gloucestershire Way).

3. Turn right, take a gate and follow the footpath at the edge of the wood, through 2 gates to a field. Follow the right fence to the corner, then cross the field ¼ right to take a gate in the fence to a drive. Turn right along the drive to the left bend, just before reaching the road, and take a gate on the right. Cross the field towards the church, turn left at a power pole to take a gate ahead and follow the track to the road. Turn left to reach Lower Swell, close to the Golden Ball Inn (Donnington Breweries).

4. Keep straight on at the road junction, passing the village green on the left. Turn right along the B4068 and left into the lane signed 'The Slaughters'. Continue for 200m and turn left along a bridle way. Follow the bridle way, cross a track to the farm, pass a barrier and continue to take a gate. Continue down hill through a narrow field with a wood on the right and take a gate. Cross the field towards Hyde Mill, cross a bridge and then take the gates to reach the buildings. Turn right and then left behind the buildings to continue along the Heart of England Way.

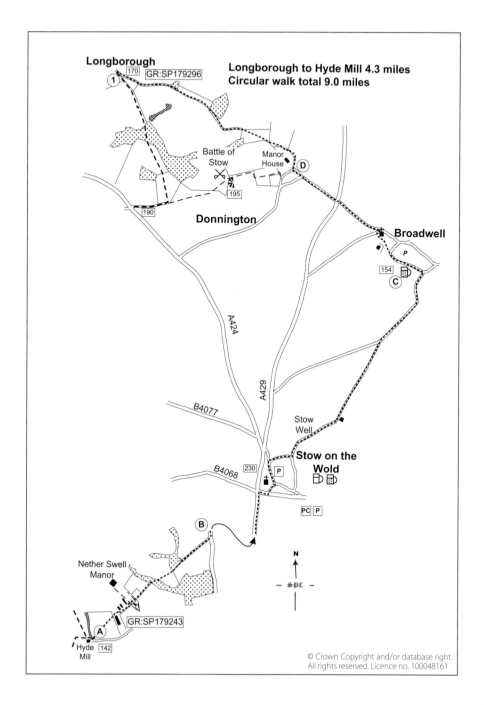

Longborough
170 GR:SP179296
1

Longborough to Hyde Mill 4.3 miles
Circular walk total 9.0 miles

Battle of
Stow
Manor
House
D
195
190

Donnington

Broadwell
P
154
C

A424

A429

B4077

Stow
Well

B4068 230 P

Stow on the
Wold

PC P

B

Nether Swell
Manor

N

GR:SP179243
A

Hyde 142
Mill

i. To visit the Battle of Stow interpretation board, take the stile to the track and then the left stile to the field. Cross the field down the slope and take a stile. Climb the hill ½ right, to the information stone.

ii. To take a short cut to Stow-on-the-Wold in the wood turn left along edge of wood and cross the bridge. Continue straight ahead across the field with the right fence and take a gate to the road. Turn right along the B4077 to follow a wide grass verge and reach Stow-on-the-Wold.

A. *At the Hyde Mill Buildings turn left through a gate and cross the mill pool bridge. Turn left and take 2 gates. Cross the field ½ left, climb the steps up the embankment and turn left through a gap in the fence. Follow the track straight ahead then, in front of the buildings, follow the footpath signs right, left and right to continue along the track. Continue up hill along the track and take 4 pairs of white gates, then cross a field with the right fence and take gate to a wood. Follow the path climbing through the wood and exit via a gate. Cross the field ½ right, take a gate and join a track to reach the road. Cross the three-lane Fosse Way with great care and turn left to Stow-on-the-Wold.*

B. *At the traffic light junction with the A436 turn right then left into Church Street. Continue to reach and turn left into the Market Square. Keep straight on joining High Street and turning right into Parsons Corner. At the Medical Practice turn left and follow the lane, down hill, passing the Stow Well. Continue to a cottage and continue left along a bridle way to reach a lane and turn right. Follow the lane to Broadwell. At the village green turn left and pass the Fox Inn (Donnington Breweries).*

C. *As the road bends right, take the footpath on the left and continue straight ahead to reach the church. Follow the path left, around the church, to the lane and turn right. At the junction turn left and follow the lane to cross the Fosse Way. Keep straight on along the road and take the 1st right to Donnington and the entrance to Donnington Manor. (See note (i) below for the level route to the Battle of Stow interpretation stone.)*

D. *From the finger post take the gate on the right. Follow the 'Ha Ha' wall around to the left and take the gate to join a track. Take a gate immediately on the right and turn left to cross a field up hill and take gate in the top corner. Cross the field down hill to take a corner gate to a bridle way track. Follow the track, take a gate, follow the left fence and rejoin a well used track up hill to reach the HoEW.*

i. *To visit the Battle of Stow interpretation stone from the finger post at the entrance to Donnington Manor turn left. Follow the lane for 100m and turn right at a footpath sign. Follow the drive to a water pump and take the gate on the left. Cross the field, take a stile and turn right and left around field perimeter. Take the stile to the interpretation stone.*

Section 32: Hyde Mill to Bourton-on-the-Water

We start on the last section of the Way at Hyde Mill and cross the River Dicker and then a natural meadow that in season has a fine display of wild flowers. Our path is now flat all along the Way as we cross the fields to reach Lower Slaughter. The village is picture perfect and the 17th century Manor House, home to a luxury Michelin star hotel and restaurant, is perhaps not the best place to find hospitality for the weary walker.

The hotel declare the name Slaughter is believed to have been the local peasants corruption of the name of the Norman Knight, Philip de Sloitre, who was first granted land here. Although the official County History has the view that Slaughter was the Saxon term for a muddy place or ditch. Next to the Manor is the church of St Mary's, but unfortunately it was re-built in 1867 so has less gravitas than many of the churches we have passed.

The Way ends in the popular tourist town of Bourton-on-the-Water, at the junction of the Oxfordshire and Gloucestershire Ways. Bourton shares its early history with Cannock Chase, where we started our journey, for Neolithic man also used the local gravel in his fire pits. Evidence of man's occupation continues throughout the ages, with evidence of a market town established in the Iron Age and later occupied by the Romans.

Today the town's main attraction is its old town centre with its many 17th century, honey-coloured, cotswold stone buildings. They provide the back cloth to the shallow River Windrush and the linear village green. This tranquil scene is perhaps less idyllic or enjoyed so well during busy summer weekends.

The return to Hyde Mill takes us quickly out of the town via the Oxfordshire Way to Greystones Farm Nature Reserve. The 18 hectare site is a Site of Special Scientific Interest through which the River Eye, which we cross, flows through. These beautiful natural meadows have the richest and largest examples of this type of habitat in the Cotswolds, with the uncommon plants that enjoy the damp meadows at their best between June and mid-July. After we have crossed the River Dickler we continue through to fields to the outskirts of Wyck Rissington.

The church of St Laurence, at the further end of the village, was consecrated in 1269 and has one of the finest examples of an early English Chancel. The church was also the home to Gustav Holst between 1892 and 1893 when, as a young man of 18, he held his first appointment here before being sent to London to study.

We continue across fields to cross the old Cheltenham to Oxford railway line, then the Fosse Way, to take the lane back to the Mill.

Walk Directions

1. Continue between the Hyde Mill buildings and the hedge towards the stone wall and take the gate on the right. Cross the field, cross the bridge and take a gate on the left. Cross the field, take a stile, continue on the same line through the hedge gap and across a ditch. Cross the field left of the corner, take a stile, cross a ditch, turn right then left with the hedge to take a gate on the right.

2. Cross the field ½ left, take twin gates across a farm access track and turn left to take a gate. Cross the field ¼ right, take a gate/stile and turn right around the corner of the field to take a gap on the right. Cross a field aiming for the end of the wood, continue with the right hedge for 300m and take a gate on the right. Turn left, follow the hedge, take a gate into a sports field, follow the track ahead, take a gate then the path to Copse Hill Road and Lower Slaughter.

3. Turn left along the road, then turn right, alongside the River Eye, to follow the bridle way signed 'Bourton-on-the-Water'. Continue along the surfaced path, crossing the river and through 2 gates to reach the Fosse Way. Turn right, cross the road at the traffic lights and turn left along Station Road. Continue past Meadow Way to turn right along a signed path, passing alongside the school, to reach High Street and turn left to the town centre and the end of the HoEW.

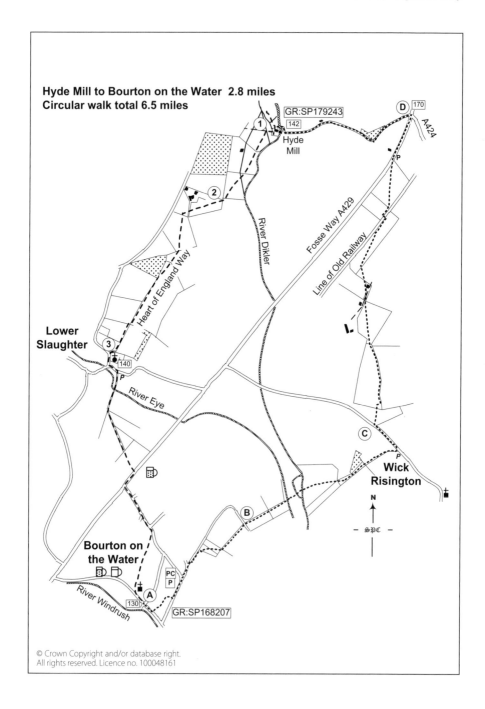

Hyde Mill to Bourton on the Water 2.8 miles
Circular walk total 6.5 miles

GR:SP179243

142

Hyde Mill

D 170

A424

River Dikler

Fosse Way A429

Line of Old Railway

Heart of England Way

Lower Slaughter

140

P

River Eye

C

Wick Risington

N

— SPC —

B

Bourton on the Water

PC
P

A

River Windrush

130

GR:SP168207

A. *To return to Hyde Mill, continue along High Street, past Moore Road and turn left along a footpath signed 'Oxfordshire Way'. Turn left along Station Road, turn right into Roman Way and right into Moor Lane. Take a gate on the right after Woodlands House. Follow the left fence, take a stile, cross a field ½ right, over a bridge, to a corner and follow the left hedge. Take a gate, cross the bridle way and take a gate into Greystone Nature Reserve.*

B. *Follow the left hedge, take a gate and continue with the left hedge. Cross a bridge, take a gate, cross a sleeper-bridge, keep straight on cross the field, cross a bridge and twin gates. Turn ½ left, through a narrow field alongside a wood, take a gate, follow the right hedge and take a gate to the road. Turn left along the road for 250m and take a gate on the right.*

C. *Cross the field ½ left, take a gate and follow the right hedge to take a gate. Cross the field ½ left, to the right of a house and take a corner gate. Turn right along the track for 10m and take a stile on the left. Turn right, follow the right fence to take a gate. Cross the field ½ left, take a gate and cross the field ½ right to turn right at a gate. Continue with the left hedge to take a gate on the left, cross the old railway line and take a gate. Turn right, continue with the right hedge, take a gate, cross the field ½ left and take a stile to the Fosse Way at a lay-by.*

D. *Cross the road to a wide grass verge and turn right to the traffic lights. Turn left along the surfaced bridle way, signed 'Hyde Mill'. Continue for 1200m to reach the Mill, crossing the bridge over the mill pond and continue to the Heart of England Way sign post.*

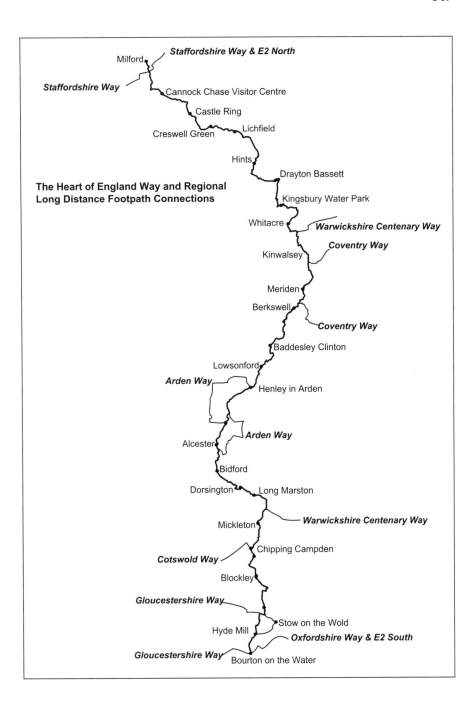

Milford

Staffordshire Way & E2 North

Staffordshire Way

Cannock Chase Visitor Centre

Castle Ring

Lichfield

Creswell Green

Hints

Drayton Bassett

**The Heart of England Way and Regional
Long Distance Footpath Connections**

Kingsbury Water Park

Whitacre

Warwickshire Centenary Way

Coventry Way

Kinwalsey

Meriden

Berkswell

Coventry Way

Baddesley Clinton

Lowsonford

Arden Way

Henley in Arden

Arden Way

Alcester

Bidford

Dorsington

Long Marston

Mickleton

Warwickshire Centenary Way

Chipping Campden

Cotswold Way

Blockley

Gloucestershire Way

Stow on the Wold

Hyde Mill

Oxfordshire Way & E2 South

Gloucestershire Way

Bourton on the Water

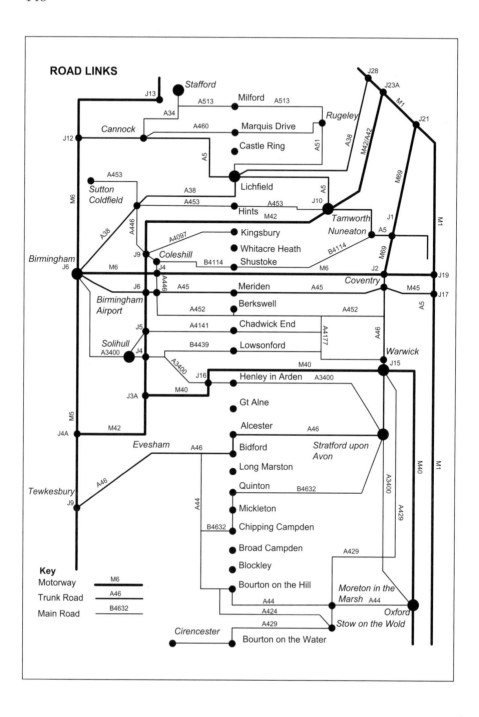

ROAD LINKS

Key
Motorway — M6
Trunk Road — A46
Main Road — B4632

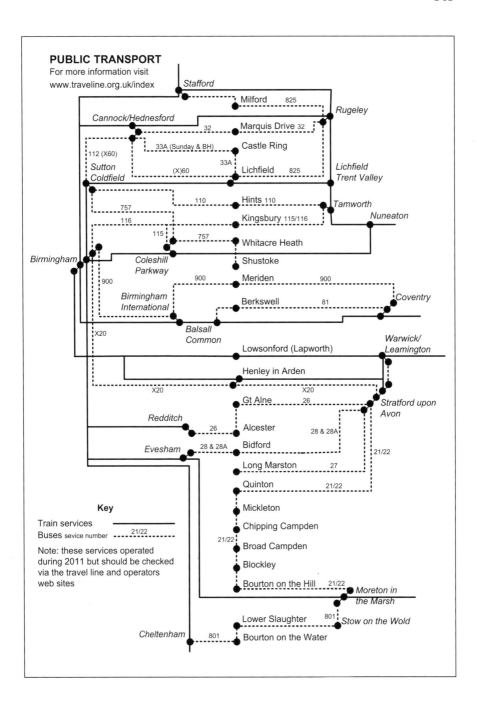

PUBLIC TRANSPORT
For more information visit
www.traveline.org.uk/index

Stafford

Milford   825

Rugeley

Cannock/Hednesford

Marquis Drive 32

32

33A (Sunday & BH)   Castle Ring

112 (X60)

Sutton
Coldfield

(X)60   33A   Lichfield   825   Lichfield
Trent Valley

110   Hints 110   Tamworth

Nuneaton

757

116   Kingsbury 115/116

115   757   Whitacre Heath

Birmingham   Coleshill   Shustoke
Parkway

900   900   Meriden   900

900   Berkswell   81   Coventry

Birmingham
International

X20   Balsall
Common

Lowsonford (Lapworth)   Warwick/
Leamington

Henley in Arden

X20   X20

Gt Alne   26   Stratford upon
Avon

Redditch

26   Alcester   28 & 28A

Evesham   28 & 28A   Bidford   21/22

Long Marston   27

Quinton   21/22

Mickleton

Key

Chipping Campden

Train services

Buses sevice number   21/22   21/22   Broad Campden

Note: these services operated
during 2011 but should be checked
via the travel line and operators
web sites

Blockley

Bourton on the Hill   21/22   Moreton in
the Marsh

Lower Slaughter   801   Stow on the Wold

Cheltenham   801   Bourton on the Water

The Arden Way – a 26 mile circular long distance footpath

The Arden Way is our other authorised footpath and is almost stile
free. The Guide book is available via our web site www.ardenway.org

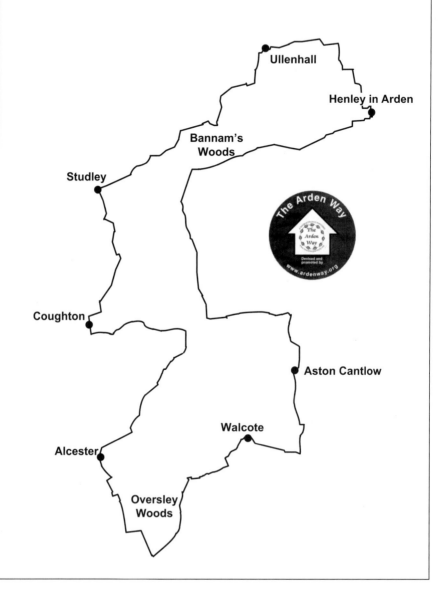

Acknowledgements

It has taken me over a year to survey and write this Guide and as with most projects there have been a few people on my team. Firstly the biggest thank you to my wife Christine, who enjoyed many of the walks with me, grinned and beared through the many hours I sat at the computer and then found the time to read every word. David Higgins, a friend of many years, who suddenly found himself with time on his hands offered to help. Between March and October, armed only with my guidance notes and maps, he has walked all of the routes. His feedback, corrections and observations have been invaluable, for which I am truly appreciative.

The Heart of England Way Association has many members who give their time as Wardens to ensure that the Way is way marked and unobstructed. I am pleased acknowledge their time together with Brian Keates who co-ordinates their efforts and was an original member of the Association. I am also pleased to record the support given to both this project and the Association by our Chairman Graham Rothery.

Finally, to my daughter Emma goes my appreciation for checking my copy and for introducing me to Bruce McAra. Bruce is a fellow walker, now in the USA, and Chief Executive Officer of Turner Townsend Inc, for whom I am grateful for their sponsorship of the Ordnance Survey copyright fee.

Become a Member of the Heart of England Way Association?

By becoming a member you will:

- Be able to join our programme of twice monthly guided walks
- Receive the twice yearly newsletter, which contains information and articles about the work of the Association and general interest articles about the countryside along the Ways.
- Ensure that the use and enjoyment of the footpaths is promoted through our Wardening and small projects programmes.

Visit our website www.heartofenglandway.org for further information about our activities and how to join.

Also from Sigma Leisure:

Country Walks in and around Wariwckshire
Ron Weston

This selection of 32 Warwickshire walks takes you on a journey of picturesque villages and historic churches, stately homes and castles, famous gardens and medieval tracks bound together by a superb network of public footpaths and canal towpaths and sometimes spilling over into adjoining counties. All walks in the book are circular, the longest being $5\frac{1}{2}$ miles and all within a radius of 25 miles from Coventry, with directions of how to get there and where to park.
£8.99

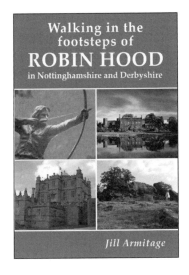

Walking in the footsteps of Robin Hood
in Nottinghamshire and Derbyshire
Jill Armitage

Walking in the Footsteps of Robin Hood roots out the places mentioned in traditional old tales and visits the locations that Robin and his men would have known. Walk through some of middle England's finest countryside on miles of well-marked footpaths to interesting historical sites associated with the outlaw legend. Stoops, caves, wells and stones with the outlaws names have been traced and woven into the walks taking you through Robin Hood country.
£8.99

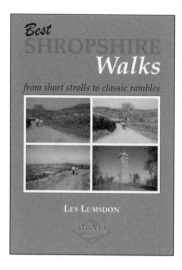

Best Shropshire Walks
from short strolls to classic routes
Les Lumsdon

The walks in this book are located in all parts of the county. Several feature fine hill walking on the Welsh borderlands, including stretches along Offa's Dyke, The Long Mynd and Caer Caradoc. Otheres start from delightful villages and hamlets in the north and east of the county, such as Acton Burnell, Myddle, Stottesdon and Welshampton. Clear maps and a selection of photographs are included.

£8.99

Walks in the Forest of Dean and Wye Valley
Dave Meredith

The Forest of Dean and Wye Valley is a paradise for both the keen rambler and the casual stroller. The 22 walks described in this book are along easy footpaths taking you to spectacular viewpoints, along woodland glades carpeted with bluebells, daffodils and foxgloves, and under the dappled shade of its golden autumn canopy.

£8.99

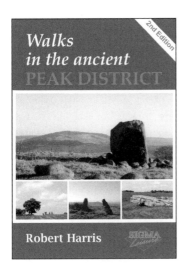

Walks in the Ancient Peak District
Robert Harris

A collection of walks visiting the prehistoric monuments and sites of the Peak District. A refreshing insight into the thinking behind the monuments, the rituals and strange behaviour of our ancestors. All the routes are circular, most starting and finishing in a town or village that is easy to locate and convenient to reach by car.

£8.99

Peak District Trigpointing Walks
Hill walking with a point to it!
Keith Stevens & Peter Whittaker

A superb introduction to an intriguing new walking experience: searching out all those elusive Ordnance Survey pillars. Packed with detailed walks to new and interesting Peak District summits, with a wealth of fascinating information on the history of the OS and the art of GPS navigation.

There are 150 Peak District Ordnance Survey pillars — can you find them all? Walk to all the best scenic viewpoints — from the top you can spot all the surrounding pillars. This book shows you how.

£8.95

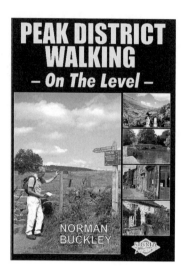

Peak District Walking On The Level
Norman Buckley

Some folk prefer easy walks, and sometimes there's just not time for an all-day yomp. In either case, this is definitely a book to keep on your bookshelf. Norman Buckley has had considerable success with "On The Level" books for the Lake District and the Yorkshire Dales.

The walks are ideal for family outings and the precise instructions ensure that there's little chance of losing your way. Well-produced maps encourage everybody to try out the walks - all of which are well scattered across the Peak District.

£7.95

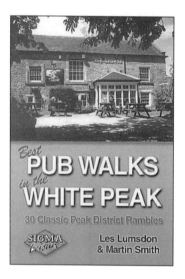

Best Pub Walks in the White Peak 30 Classic Peak District Rambles
Les Lumsden & Martin Smith

The 30 fabulous walks range from three to nine miles and ideal for family rambles. They start in such delightful Peak District villages as Ashford-in-the-Water, Alstonefield and Youlgreave, most of which are accessible by public transport — so that you can leave the car at home and savour the products on offer at the authors' favourite pubs.

Follow the recommendatios in this well-established — and completely updated — book for a superb variety of walks in splendid scenery and, after each walk, relax in a Peak District pub renowned for its welcome to walkers and for the quality of its Real Ale, often supplied by local independent brewers.

£8.99

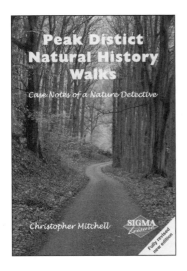

Peak District Walking Natural History Walks
Christopher Mitchell

An updated 2nd Edition with 18 varied walks for all lovers of the great outdoors — and armchair ramblers too! Learn how to be a nature detective, a 'case notes' approach shows you what clues to look for and how to solve them. Detailed maps include animal tracks and signs, landscape features and everything you need for the perfect natural history walk. There are mysteries and puzzles to solve to add more fun for family walks — solutions supplied! Includes follow on material with an extensive Bibliography and 'Taking it Further' sections.

£8.99

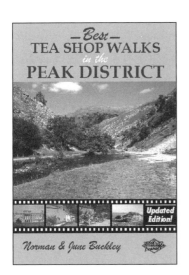

Best Tea Shop Walks in the Peak District
Norman and June Buckley

A wonderful collection of easy-going walks that are ideal for families and all those who appreciate fine scenery with a touch of decandence in the shape of an afternoon tea or morning coffee —or both! The 26 walks are spread widely across the Peak District, including Lyme Park, Castleton, Miller's Dale, and The Roaches and — of course — such famous dales as Lathkill and Dovedale. Each walk has a handy summary so that you can choose the walks that are ideally suited to the interests and abilities of your party. The tea shops are just as diverse, ranging from the splendour of Chatsworth House to more basic locations. Each one welcomes ramblers and there is always a good choice of tempting goodies.

£8.99

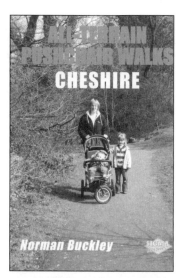
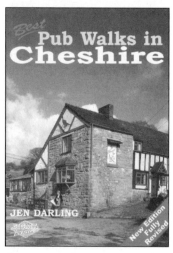